INTO THE CLOUDS

THE RACE TO CLIMB THE WORLD'S
MOST DANGEROUS MOUNTAIN

TOD OLSON

SCHOLASTIC INC.

To the Children of the Belay

Table of Contents

K2, the second-highest mountain on Earth, rises more than 5 miles above sea level.

Prologue

Camp VIII, K2, August 6, 1953

All they needed were three good days. Three days without winds strong enough to blow them off the mountainside. Three days without those tiny ice crystals that filled the air so thoroughly they had to cover their mouths with a mitten to breathe. Three days of weather clear enough to see the route between their lonely tents and the top of the second-highest mountain on Earth.

On the afternoon of August 6, 1953, Charlie Houston knew those three days might not come soon enough. He was a doctor in his other life, 7,000 miles away in New Hampshire. Now, in the relative shelter of their tents, he examined his climbing partners one by one. When he made George Bell take his boots off, he could see that two toes were starting to blacken from frostbite. Bob Craig didn't look much better. There were nasty spots on his heels, the first sign that ice crystals were forming in the flesh. Dee Molenaar was struggling, too. He had lost at least 30 pounds since leaving home three months ago. He had a painful sore throat, and his right foot had turned blue and itchy in places.

Outside the tents, the wind howled. Snow blew sideways through the air. Fresh white powder piled up on the mountainside. Some slopes held tons of the stuff, ready to avalanche thousands of feet to the valley with one misplaced boot. Climbing was out of the question. During the worst of the storm, just walking from tent to tent felt like too big a risk.

It was maddening, really. Twice before, Houston had been within a day's climb of one of Earth's highest summits. And still he hadn't made it.

Now he was within reach again. For six days the team had been camped on a shoulder of the mountain known as K2. They were eight men packed into three tents, 25,000 feet above the Asian nation of Pakistan.

Three thousand feet above them stood the summit. No one on Earth had ever set foot there. Seven weeks of painstaking work had gotten them to this nearly level sliver of ground. But once they arrived, the sky had closed in on them.

Day after day, blizzard conditions hid both the summit above and the valley below. They still had radio contact with Base Camp. But that weak voice scratching through their speaker was the only sign of the world below.

Camp VIII, high above the highway-like tracks of two glaciers.

Otherwise, it felt to Houston like they were the only people in existence.

Some days had been so brutal they'd barely left their sleeping bags. But even then, the cold stalked them. It forced its way through the tent walls, through the insulated down bags, through layers of wool and cotton and nylon. No matter how deep they burrowed, they never got warm.

They did what they could to keep from going crazy with boredom. Sometimes, Houston's longtime friend and climbing partner, Bob Bates, read to the rest of them. Sometimes they just lay there while the wind-whipped tent walls slapped at their shoulders and heads.

Mostly, they planned their push to the summit.

The day before, on August 5, they had picked the summit teams by secret vote—two pairs of climbers who would set out as soon as the weather broke. Both teams were prepared never to reveal that they had been to the top of the

The team, with the flag they hoped to place on the summit. Left to right: Bob Bates, Tony Streather, Charlie Houston, Dee Molenaar, George Bell, Bob Craig.

world. If they succeeded, the expedition's official announcement would say only, "Two men reached the top." Houston wanted the entire team to get credit.

It was the way he had planned it from the start. To Houston, climbing was teamwork—"the fellowship of the rope," he called it. On the mountain, they climbed tied together at the waist, bound in a partnership. If one climber fell, the other could be swept a mile down a mountainside to his death. Or he could save his partner's life with an ice axe, jammed into the snow at the last possible moment. The climbers held each other's lives in hand. They succeeded together or failed together.

Too often it didn't happen that way. Fourteen years earlier, just a few hundred feet below Houston's high camp, an American climber named Dudley Wolfe lay in a tent, alone and dying. His expedition had fallen apart. Most of the party sat at Base Camp, recovering from exhaustion and altitude sickness. In the chaos, Wolfe had been left behind. Three climbers from Nepal struggled back up the mountain and tried to reach him in a howling storm. The four men were never seen again.

By 1953, all trace of Wolfe's final camp had been swept from the mountain. But no one in Houston's expedition had forgotten his story.

▲

When Houston's team began to poke their heads outside the tents on August 7, the weather looked promising. The wind had calmed a bit. Skies were overcast, but the clouds hung high. Visibility was good enough for climbing. The mountain, it seemed, had finally given them a break.

In the morning light, the men began to stumble around in the snow. To Houston they looked like castaways from a shipwreck just reaching shore.

Bob Craig emerged from his tent. If the weather held, it looked like he and Pete Schoening, the youngest of them all, might make a dash for the summit.

Craig was standing outside his tent, fumbling with his camera, when he saw Art Gilkey come out into the light. More than anyone else on the team, Gilkey had his heart set on reaching the top of K2. He'd been complaining of leg cramps for a couple of days, but he'd proven himself strong enough to be voted onto the second summit team.

Craig was about to snap a photo when Gilkey stumbled and collapsed in the snow.

The climbers made their way to their fallen teammate as fast as they could. It looked like Gilkey had passed out for a moment, but he lifted his head and said, "I'm all right. It's just my leg, that's all."

In fact, he was far from all right.

They pulled Gilkey up and half dragged him back into his tent. Houston helped him peel off a couple of layers of clothing and did not like what he saw. Gilkey's left ankle was red, swollen, and painful to the touch. The skin felt warm.

Gilkey looked at Houston hopefully. "It's sure to clear up in another day, isn't it?"

Houston could hear the doubt in his climbing partner's voice. There may have been a hint of desperation, too. Mumbling some words of reassurance, Houston wrapped both of Gilkey's calves tightly. Then he excused himself and went back to the others to report the bad news.

Gilkey, Houston said, had developed clots in the veins of his left calf, blocking his circulation. Even with perfect blood flow, the extreme cold put limbs at risk. Without it, Gilkey's leg was in dire trouble. "What's more," Houston went on, "sometimes bits of clot break off and are carried to the lungs. At sea level, it's often fatal. Up here . . ." Houston trailed off, not wanting to finish the thought.

It was every climber's nightmare, becoming disabled near the top of a mountain. And the moment it became apparent was full of unasked questions. If Gilkey truly couldn't climb, there was only one way for him to get down: Houston, Bates, and the others would have to carry him. That was a task that would put each of them near the edge of death.

No humans had ever spent this much time this high above sea level and survived. For a week now, they had been on the edge of what climbers call the Death Zone. As a doctor, Houston knew exactly what that meant. For seven days they had been breathing air without enough oxygen in it. Their bodies and their brains were slowly dying. Every step took extreme effort. The simplest decisions required intense concentration.

Each climber barely had the strength to be responsible for himself. How could they possibly get Art Gilkey down alive?

PART ONE

1938

The Dirty Work

The First American Karakoram Expedition
Standing from second to left: Bill House, Charlie Houston
(pronounced *how-ston*), Norman Streatfeild, Paul Petzoldt, Bob Bates, Dick
Burdsall. Seated: Ang Pemba, Phinsoo,
Pasang Kikuli, Pemba Kitar, Tse Tendrup, Sonam.

1

Because It's There

The mountain that held Charlie Houston and his team of climbers high on its slopes was born millions of years ago in a collision that reshaped the face of the Earth. The landmass we call India lay far off the southern coast of Asia. As the Earth's crust shifted beneath it, the Indian continent edged northward through the ocean. While it traveled, dinosaurs went extinct, an ice age came and went, apes began walking on two legs and evolved into humans.

This massive continent plowed into the rest of Asia 50 million years before Houston's expedition. It slowed but didn't stop. One giant landmass ground into another. Over millions of years, the land thrust toward the sky and created the highest mountains on Earth.

They're known as the Himalaya—"abode of snow" in the Sanskrit language of India—and there is nothing on the globe that compares to them. The mountains range along China's border with Pakistan, India, Nepal, and Bhutan.

Thirty-seven of them tower more than 25,000 feet above sea level. Twelve rise more than five miles into the sky. The tallest mountain outside of Asia is the 22,841-foot-high Aconcagua in Argentina. Move it to the Himalaya and it wouldn't rank in the top 200. "Most mountains are of the Earth," wrote John Kenneth Galbraith, an American ambassador to India. "The Himalayas belong to the heavens."

▲

A few thousand years ago—just a sliver in the timeline of a mountain's life—humans began to build homes in the shadow of the Himalayan summits. These villagers hunted in the foothills of the mountains. They used frigid river water to coax barley and wheat out of the soil. They carried heavy loads through low mountain passes to trade in other lands. They learned to call the mountains home.

Never, as far as we know, did they try to climb to the top.

Who, after all, would want to? On the high slopes of the Himalaya, there is no such thing as summer. Snow and ice smother massive slabs of rock all year round. Winds whip the summits at speeds over 100 miles an hour. Nothing grows. And nothing survives for long.

Like Galbraith, the people of the Himalaya were convinced that the high peaks didn't belong to humans. The mountains were the home of the gods. And the gods did not want visitors. In 1830, a British official named G. W.

INTO THE CLOUDS

Traill stumbled out of the Himalaya after one of the earliest Western expeditions there. The glare from the snow had turned his eyes swollen and raw. The locals who greeted him decided that the mountain goddess had struck him blind for trespassing. Legend has it she took pity on Traill and restored his sight—after he made a cash offering at a nearby temple.

Wanderers in the mountains—traders, warriors, and religious missionaries—warned about other dangers lurking in the snow and ice. Some people told stories of a giant, two-legged snowman known as a Yeti. In the 600s, the Buddhist missionary Xuanzang returned to China from a Himalayan journey with this advice: "Travelers are often attacked by fierce dragons so they should neither wear red

The Himalaya, from the top of a peak in India.

garments nor carry gourds with them, nor shout loudly," he warned. "Even the slightest violation of these rules will invite disaster."

But gods and mythological creatures weren't the only forces keeping people off the high peaks. Travelers also noticed a more earthbound hazard: People who climbed too high on the slopes got sick. "Men's bodies become feverish, they lose color, and are attacked with headache and vomiting; the asses and cattle being all in like condition," warned a Chinese general in AD 20. In fact, the peaks had been named for their hazards. There was "Mount Greater Headache," "Mount Lesser Headache," and "Fever Hill."

Almost 2,000 years after the general's observation, science solved the mystery of Mount Greater Headache. The

problem at the very top of the world is that breathing no longer does the body much good. As the mountain slopes rise, gravity fades and releases its pressure. The molecules that make up air—mostly nitrogen and oxygen—float farther and farther apart. Every breath taken at the top of the Himalaya has one-third the oxygen of a breath taken on the shore of the ocean. That's not enough to keep a human alive for long.

In 1953, a Swiss doctor named Edward Wyss-Dunant drew an imaginary line at 25,500 feet above sea level. "Life there is impossible," he wrote, "and it requires the whole of a man's will to maintain himself there for a few days." He called this region the "death zone."

The Earth has plenty of unwelcoming places. But humans have learned to live in most of them. Nomadic people inhabit the desert, moving from watering hole to watering hole. A research station sits atop the South Pole, and scientists huddle there through the winter. The high peaks of the Himalaya may be the only land area on the globe where humans simply can't survive.

It might as well be another planet.

▲

Humans started exploring the Himalayan summits for the same reason they learned to blast themselves into space. They didn't want their enemies to get there first.

In the 1700s, the British came to India to make money.

Merchants from the British East India Company traded for spices, tea, and textiles in the Himalayan foothills. Before long, they had an army supporting them. British governors took over India from Calcutta to Kashmir—2,000 miles along the southwestern border of the highest mountains in the world.

Right behind the merchants and the soldiers and the governors came the surveyors, eager to stake out the boundaries of the empire. They hired local porters to lug their equipment up the mountainsides. From there they mapped the valleys and measured the peaks. They even recruited Indian spies, known as pundits, to explore the hidden passes of the Himalaya. Their job was to watch for Russians making their way across the spine of the mountains from the north.

In the late 1800s, a new kind of climber arrived in the Himalaya. These men (they were nearly all men) came from Europe and sometimes the United States. On some expeditions, they had surveyors or soldiers with them. But they went to the mountains not to make maps or extend empires. They climbed for the sheer challenge of setting foot on one of the most inaccessible places on Earth.

"If I am asked what is the use of climbing," said Francis Younghusband, who was both a soldier and a mountaineer, "I reply, No use at all: no more use than kicking a football about, or dancing, or playing the piano, or writing a poem, or painting a picture." Climbing to the top of the world would "elevate the human spirit," he believed. It would prove that humans were "getting the upper hand on the earth [and] acquiring a true mastery of their surroundings."

But more often than not, it was the mountains that got the upper hand. That became clear right at the start. In 1895, a British mountaineer named Albert Frederick Mummery set out to climb Nanga Parbat, at the western edge of the Himalaya. Mummery had mastered the rock and ice walls of the Swiss Alps, and when he first saw Nanga Parbat, he was convinced it wouldn't be much harder.

He was wrong.

Nanga Parbat's summit stood 26,600 feet above the sea, more than 10,000 feet higher than any peak in the Alps. Mummery and his climbing partners spent a month trying various routes until the mountain left them one final chance to reach the top—a steep, icy wall called the Rakhiot Face. Mummery's climbing partners opted for a safe but round-about route to the base of the wall. But Mummery was impatient with the mountain. On August 24, he took two Indian porters on a shortcut through a high mountain pass. The three men were never seen again.

▲

The deaths of Mummery and his Indian companions didn't stop the new breed of mountaineers. Fourteen peaks in the Himalaya stood higher than 8,000 meters (26,247 feet), and they became the coveted prizes in a race to the top of the world. Climbers paid for their expeditions in part by selling their stories to newspapers and magazines. Back home, Europeans and Americans devoured the tales of adventure. The names of the mountains rang with mystery: Cho Oyu, Dhaulagiri, Makalu, and Gasherbrum. The public was fascinated by the danger.

In 1921, the magazine *Lady's Pictorial* published a breathless article about one of the first attempts on Everest, the tallest mountain of all. "Who first faces and triumphs over the intense cold, avalanches, terrific winds, blinding snowstorms, loneliness, and unknown other perils of this mountain of mystery and magic will be forever famous. What an adventure! What a thrilling story to tell!" Before running out of exclamation points, the writer added, "But, alas! What certain sacrifice of life must be made in the effort."

Everest had become the great challenge in the Himalaya, and in 1924, a British climber named George Mallory nearly fought his way to the top. But he and his climbing partner vanished 800 feet below the summit. Before his final expedition, Mallory had given a cryptic answer to the question every climber had to field. When a reporter asked him why he wanted to climb Everest, he replied, "Because it's there."

By 1938, none of the 8,000-meter peaks had been

WAS THE SUMMIT OF EVEREST REACHED?

Mr. Odell's Story, which is Now Being Told from the Lecture Platform

Copyrighted in the U.S.A.

Drawn by D. Macpherson from personal description by N. E. Odell

THE LAST PHASE OF THE EXPEDITION—IRVINE AND MALLORY SCALING THE FINAL HEIGHTS TOWARDS "THE CITADEL," WHICH, INDEED, THEY MAY ACTUALLY HAVE REACHED

A magazine article from 1924 wondering if Mallory and his climbing partner, Andrew Irvine, made it to the summit of Everest before they vanished.

climbed. Seven expeditions had attempted Everest and seven had failed. Twelve people had died trying. In 1934, a German expedition to Nanga Parbat had fallen apart in a devastating storm. Nine climbers died trying to make it back down the mountain. Just two years later, an avalanche tumbled from the heights of the same peak, smothering 16 climbers in their camp.

An article appeared in the *New York Times* in April of 1938, once again wondering why climbers seemed to be so obsessed with such a dangerous pursuit. "[Mankind] has the notion that he can't rightly claim title to his planet till he has walked over all of its surface that will bear his weight. He has put his heel on the poles, the continental ice caps, the lonely jungles and deserts and the loftiest peaks of Europe, the Americas and Africa. The last great unknowns left for him on earth are the still untrodden mountain tops in the heart of Asia."

That article also announced a new expedition, not to Everest but to the second-highest mountain in the world. This peak was about as unknown as any place on Earth. It stood tucked away in the far northern reaches of the Himalaya. It was so hard to get to that only two expeditions had even attempted to climb it.

The mountain was K2, and the leader of the expedition was a 24-year-old medical student named Charlie Houston.

Houston had been keeping a journal since he started

planning the expedition, and he'd been thinking about his own reasons for climbing. "Is it not better to take risks . . . than die within from rot? Is it not better to change one's life completely than to wait for the brain to set firmly and irreversibly in one way of life and one environment? I think it is . . . taking risks, not for the sake of danger alone, but for the sake of growth, is more important than any security one can buy or inherit."

It would be another 15 years before Houston attempted one of the riskiest operations in the history of mountaineering: getting Art Gilkey down from 25,000 feet. But that story begins here, in 1938, as Charlie Houston prepared to lead his first K2 expedition across the Atlantic Ocean into the heart of the Himalaya.

2

Not Like Other Mountains

The three men circled the overturned wastebasket and circled it again, trying to imagine the real mountain. It was the closest they could come at the moment—photos of K2 from all angles leaning against a trash can in the New York Public Library.

It was early spring 1938, and Charlie Houston was looking for a route to K2's 28,250-foot-high summit. Houston was just finishing his second year of medical school. And he was about to lead a major American expedition to the Himalaya.

Houston, Bob Bates, and a talented climber named Bill House had assembled the photos around the wastebasket. They leaned in, studying every ridge and every gulley. How steep were the snow slopes? What was ice and what was rock? Where was the route blocked by jutting cliffs or overhanging ice?

Officially, the expedition wasn't supposed to make it all

Houston, House, and Bates studied photos taken by the famous Italian photographer Vittorio Sella on a 1909 expedition. Here, porters from Sella's expedition leave K2 after their unsuccessful attempt to climb the mountain.

the way to the top of the mountain. Their job was to find the best route to the summit and report back. The following year, Fritz Wiessner planned to follow in their footsteps. He would use Houston's scouting work to make his way up K2. If everything went according to plan, Wiessner would go down in history as the first person to stand on the summit.

That, at least, was the goal of the American Alpine Club (AAC), the group that coordinated the expeditions. Charlie Houston wasn't at all sure how he felt about it.

Like most mountaineers, Houston had a lot of respect for Wiessner's climbing skills. At 38, Wiessner had solved some of the hardest routes in the world, often without ropes.

But Wiessner was also fiercely competitive, and he had his eye on the summit of K2. Houston suspected he was in it mostly for the money and the glory. At one point, Wiessner had told Houston that if he conquered K2, he would be "set for life." Wiessner had also written to the head of the AAC, asking him to remind Houston not to be "reckless" in pursuit of a "brilliant success."

Houston and Bates thought they understood the real message: Wiessner wanted to make sure no one beat him to the top of K2. "Wiessner's idea, I suppose is to have us do the . . . dirty work," Bates wrote to a friend, "then go in next year and profit by our mistakes."

Houston and Bates had no desire to be reckless. But they also didn't want to get stuck doing the dirty work. If they got close, why shouldn't they try for the summit?

Just two years before, Houston had been close to another summit in the Himalaya. He and a climbing partner made it to 25,000 feet on Nanda Devi, just a few hundred feet below the summit. The two men scouted a route to the top for the following day. Then they returned to camp and cracked open a can of corned beef to celebrate. Two hours later, Houston was crawling over his partner to vomit out the door of the tent.

The next day, he limped down to a lower camp, wiped out by food poisoning. Another teammate replaced him and made it to the top two days later. It was the highest mountain climbed to date, and all Houston could do was lie in his sleeping bag and listen to the story when his partners returned. He was thrilled to be a part of the expedition, but still—if not for a single can of spoiled meat, it would have been him standing on the summit.

Now, another chance lay in front of Houston. He may not have appreciated Wiessner's single-minded focus on the summit. But like all Himalayan climbers, he dreamed of looking down from one of the world's highest peaks.

That day in the library, however, as Houston, Bates, and House circled their two-dimensional mountain, they couldn't see a path to the top. On all sides of the wastebasket, K2 looked the same—a jagged, unyielding, hopelessly steep pyramid of rock, snow, and ice. Even in pictures, it looked impossible to climb.

▲

Of all the mountains in the world, Everest gets most of the attention. But to mountaineers, K2 is the bigger challenge. It lies hidden deep in a part of the Himalaya known as the Karakoram, or "black rock." The name comes from the millions of tons of dark boulders, stones, and pebbles that have tumbled from the peaks to the ice-clogged valleys below.

In the 1850s, British surveyors slogged through India to the Karakoram as part of their effort to mark the borders of their empire. An army lieutenant named Thomas Montgomerie climbed a ridge and started counting peaks. His imagination apparently exhausted by the trek, he labeled them all with a K (for Karakoram) and a number. By the time he was done, he had 32 peaks marked on his map: K1 all the way to K32. Most of the mountains eventually took their local names—Gasherbrum and Chogolisa and Distaghil Sar. But K2 was so far from the nearest village that it didn't have a widely accepted name.

Alone among the mountains of the Karakoram, K2 kept its industrial-sounding label. "Just the bare bones of a name," an Italian climber would later write. "All rock and ice and storm and abyss. It makes no attempt to sound human."

And the mountain itself hasn't been welcoming to the humans who have tried to climb it. Everest stands 750 feet higher, but K2 is more treacherous. Its slopes are relentlessly steep. Its weather is unpredictable. Fifty-mile-per-hour winds batter its flanks regularly. In the winter it can feel like -100 degrees Fahrenheit near the summit.

Today, more than 9,000 climbers have reached the top of Everest. Fewer than 400 have successfully climbed K2. For every four mountaineers who have stood on its summit, one has died trying to get there. Climbers have frozen to death on its icy slopes. They have been swept away by avalanches of ice and snow. They have been blown by gale-force winds off its summit ridge into the valley 10,000 feet below.

Before 1938, only two serious expeditions had tried to climb K2. Neither of them made it higher than 22,000 feet.

The second of those expeditions marched through the Karakoram in 1909, led by an Italian nobleman known as the Duke of Abruzzi. A line of 250 porters trudged behind the Italians, carrying ten-and-a-half tons of food and equipment. But no amount of supplies could get them near the summit. "The simple fact is that these are not mountains like other mountains," concluded the expedition's doctor, "and one cannot look at them without disquiet and foreboding."

The duke returned to Italy convinced that K2 could not

The Duke of Abruzzi's expedition on its approach to K2. The photographer Sella is on the right.

be climbed. "If anyone does get to the top," he told the Italian Alpine Club, "it will be a pilot and not a mountaineer."

▲

On May 9, 1938, Charlie Houston stepped out of a train in Rawalpindi, India. There were no pilots in sight—only mountaineers. Bob Bates and Bill House, his two companions from the wastebasket planning session, were there to meet him. So were three other members of the expedition: a hulking mountain guide from Wyoming named Paul Petzoldt, a 42-year-old engineer named Dick Burdsall, and an Englishman named Norman Streatfeild. Houston had stayed behind to finish his medical school exams and was just catching up to the team now.

In Rawalpindi, Houston also greeted his old friend Pasang Kikuli. Kikuli had been hired, at Houston's request, to lead the group of Sherpas that would serve as the backbone of the expedition.

Kikuli's Sherpa ancestors had lived in the foothills of the Himalaya for hundreds of years. When the first Western climbers came to the area, Sherpas found work carrying expedition gear to the mountains. They packed and unpacked tents, carried heavy loads, and called their Western employers sahib—a term that translates roughly as "sir."

Often, the Western climbers treated their helpers as servants. But Sherpas like Kikuli, Angtharkay, Pasang Lama, and Gaylay were quickly learning to climb as well as their employers. They rarely got the credit, but without them, many expeditions wouldn't have gotten halfway up the mountain.

By 1938, Kikuli already had a reputation as one of the finest Sherpa climbers around. He had survived the deadly 1934 expedition to Nanga Parbat, when a nine-day storm

A Sherpa porter, flanked by two British climbers, hauls a load up the slopes of Everest during a 1933 expedition.

stranded a German team high on the mountain. Three German climbers and six Sherpas died from starvation and hypothermia trying to get down. Kikuli got away with his life. But his feet were badly damaged from frostbite.

Two years later he went to Nanda Devi with Houston. On that trip, he went snow-blind from the relentless white glare and never made it above Camp II. But he and Houston became close friends on the expedition. Houston was happy to have him back on the way to K2.

Paul Petzoldt, he wasn't so sure about. Houston worried from the start that the big man wouldn't fit in with the rest of the team. Houston and the others had gone to expensive colleges. They read poetry to each other at night in the tents. Petzoldt, on the other hand, had no college degree. He was a mountain guide from the western U.S., a long way from the wealthy neighborhoods where the rest of them had grown up.

For his part, Petzoldt felt the rest of the party were "amateurs." He was convinced they should be paying him to guide them up the mountain.

Houston and Petzoldt also had some heated debates over how to climb. Houston was a purist. He hated protective equipment like pitons—the metal spikes that climbers pounded into the mountain to protect themselves on dangerous pitches. The true mountaineer, he insisted, climbed with as little equipment as possible. Climbers who ran ropes from piton to piton and hauled themselves up turned an adventure into an engineering task.

Petzoldt, on the other hand, had no problem with a little hardware if it kept him from falling off a mountainside. At the beginning of the trip, he'd been appalled to find that Houston had packed only 10 pitons. He bought a stash of 50 more on the way to India and tucked them away. He'd never been to K2, but he'd seen pictures. There were places where one bad step could launch you down the mountain. You could easily fall 10,000 feet before you'd land.

On May 10, with a few extra pounds of pitons clanking around, the climbers loaded two trucks with supplies and headed for the foothills of the Himalaya.

3

From Another World

For a Himalayan expedition, Houston's party traveled light. Even so, they had two tons of food and supplies, all shipped in large tea chests from New York to India. There were tinted snow goggles, down sleeping bags, tents, and coils of rope. There were leather boots with short nails driven through the soles for traction and spiked attachments known as crampons for kicking footholds into snow and ice.

To keep themselves fed on the mountain, they packed dried vegetables, fruit, and powdered milk. They carried hot cereal, canned meats, and biscuits. For the high altitudes, they reserved 50 pounds of pemmican—a high-calorie mixture of dried meat, grain, and raisins used by polar explorers on expeditions to Antarctica and the Arctic.

Before they left home, Bob Bates had run the food through tests that sometimes involved more than tasting. To find the perfect kind of biscuits, he dropped them from a second-story window. Then he left them out in the rain for a night. The winning brand had to stand up to moisture without getting soggy but break into pieces without help from a hacksaw.

In India the men selected extra climbing rope with an equally practical test. They went from shop to shop, picked out rope that looked like the right thickness, and slung a length of it over a ceiling beam. Sensing entertainment, crowds of local boys gathered while the climbers grabbed the rope and hung from it. Most of the selections held Bates and House just fine. But when the brawny Petzoldt jumped on, the ropes snapped. The three of them went sprawling on the floor, sending their audience into hysterics. It took a few tries before they found a rope that would hold all of them.

▲

Once they had their gear together, hauling it to K2 was like a major military operation. They had traveled 8,000 miles by ship to Bombay, India; 1,000 miles by train across a desert to Rawalpindi; and 100 miles by truck to the town of Srinagar in the foothills of the mountains. There, they split the supplies into 50-pound loads. After one more 18-mile truck ride, they left the luxury of wheels behind for good.

They still had 330 miles to go.

Ponies carried their gear for the first half of the trek,

driven by local men from the region of Baltistan. The caravan slogged through valleys battered by avalanches—snow and rock and massive tree trunks, all tossed from the peaks above them.

Just past the Balti capital of Skardu, the terrain grew too rugged for horses. Streatfeild, the expedition's transport officer, hired 44 porters and pressed ahead. The Balti porters made their way along narrow ledges with 50-pound loads threatening to pull them off. Rivers swollen with meltwater from the mountain peaks raged hundreds of feet below.

But climbing high above the rivers was nothing compared to crossing them. As they approached the last village on their route, they came face-to-face with the infamous Balti rope bridge. The bridges were made from willow twigs, braided together into six-inch-thick cables, one for the feet and two "railings" for the hands.

These treacherous bridges formed a final gateway to K2, as though they were meant to weed out the unworthy. Houston, Bates, and the rest had heard stories about them—every mountaineer had. Two climbers once flipped a bridge over and dangled above a churning river for several minutes before they could be rescued. Another man was so terrified of the crossing that he had to be blindfolded and carried over by a porter. Rumor had it that the

Baltis didn't give the bridges regular maintenance. They waited until each one broke to fix it.

Bates stepped onto the trembling ropes, wondering how the last person to reveal a flaw had fared. "At every step the rope contraption squeaked a protest and tremors bounded along the foot cable," he recalled later. He edged along, watching each step to make sure his feet landed squarely on the rope. That, however, made it impossible to ignore the churning water below.

One by one, the climbers stepped back onto solid ground, where the porters greeted them with smiles. Most of the Baltis had raced across the bridge, even with their 50-pound packs. They must have found it amusing to watch the famed American mountaineers, carrying only small day sacks, inch across the ropes, fearing for their lives.

A week later, the expedition trudged up the Godwin-Austen Glacier—a huge pathway of ice, covered in snow and fallen rock, that weaves through the Karakoram to the doorstep of K2. Low clouds hung over the broad, gray surface of the ice. The men plodded along blindly. Suddenly, a window of clear sky opened. A gleaming, ghostly pyramid of snow and ice appeared less than 10 miles away, hanging impossibly high in the sky. It was their first glimpse of the peak they had come to climb.

Houston and the others stopped in their tracks, stunned.

Climbers from the 1939 expedition negotiating the same rope bridges Houston's team faced in 1938.

In a moment, the clouds shifted and the mountain was gone, as though it had never existed. To Bates, "It was like something from another world, something ethereal seen in a dream."

▲

By June 12, K2 was more than a dream. It was a solid mass of rock, ice, and snow under the boots of 12 men. The Balti porters had gone home with orders to return in six weeks. Their 50-pound loads lay in piles at the foot of the mountain where the Sherpas and the six sahibs set up their Base Camp.

With their tents pitched, the climbers stared up at the mountain, trying to imagine the route that would unlock its summit. A giant pyramid loomed over them, its sides far from smooth. Huge spurs, or ridges, ran from the base of K2 nearly to the summit. They stood out like bony spines on a reptile.

The ridges looked terrifying. They peaked in knife-edged crests that dropped off thousands of feet to the glaciers below. But those craggy spines were the only safe route up the mountain. Climbers who tried to ascend the low gullies between the ridges invited disaster. The gullies were funnels for giant avalanches—thousands of tons of ice and snow tumbling from the heights faster than a speeding train.

A ridge it would have to be—but which one? They needed a route free from impossibly steep barriers of rock and ice,

Three of the expedition's Sherpa climbers watching an avalanche on the west face of K2.

a route that would not bury them in avalanching snow. And somewhere on this unyielding mountainside, they needed to find a route with a few places level enough to pitch tents.

A mountain as big as K2 couldn't be climbed in a mad rush to the top. The human body needed time to acclimatize—to get used to the changing altitude. That became clear enough in 1875, when three French balloonists decided to test their performance at great heights. They soared to 28,000 feet—about the height of K2—in less than four hours. When they returned to Earth, two of them were dead, their faces blackened from lack of oxygen.

The effects of altitude were at least somewhat predictable. The weather was not, and it gave Houston and his teammates another reason to advance carefully. If a storm rolled in, they could be trapped on the mountain for days at a time. To give themselves refuge, they would make a chain of camps up the slope, and stock them with supplies by ferrying loads from below. Each camp required a tiny piece of ground flat enough to keep tents from sliding off the mountain.

With their strategy clear, Houston, Bates, House, Petzoldt, Burdsall, and Streatfeild split into teams and probed at the mountain. Kikuli and the Sherpas followed in their footsteps with heavy loads on their backs. They had the Duke of Abruzzi's notes to guide them. They had nearly memorized the photos from the wastebasket session. And yet, none of it seemed to help.

On the northwest ridge, Houston and House ran into a steep, 800-foot snow slope with ice an inch beneath the surface. They would have to hack steps into the slope with ice axes at 21,000 feet. One slip and they'd hurtle 4,000 feet down the ridge. Even if they could manage, it would be too risky for the Sherpas carrying 40-pound loads.

A quarter of the way around the mountain, the northeast ridge was no better. Houston, Bates, and Burdsall spied a massive pinnacle. It hung over the upper part of the spur like a guard tower, waiting to drop deadly chunks of ice on anyone who dared attack the ridge.

And the south face of the mountain? It was nothing but steep slopes loaded with unstable snow. They'd be buried alive before they made it halfway up.

That left the spur the duke gave his name to—the Abruzzi Ridge—before leaving the mountain in defeat. Houston and House scouted the ridge. It looked climbable, but they saw nowhere to pitch a tent. They did find a few pieces of wood at around 18,000 feet, left over from one of the duke's crates. It was not far from there that the Duke of Abruzzi had turned around, deciding once and for all that you needed wings to reach the top of K2.

▲

A deep depression fell over the camp. June was coming to an end. They'd been on the mountain for two weeks and they were no closer to finding a way up. In their frustration, the team members started to snipe at each other. House was a great climber, but Houston felt he didn't do his share of the work. Instead, House and Petzoldt complained about the food rations. They were sick of corn and hash and kept demanding the pemmican that Houston was saving for the high altitudes. "Bob and I very mad," Houston wrote in his diary on June 22, "gave them leftover ½ tin and swore."

But on July 2, it was Petzoldt and House who found the expedition's first foothold on the route. They were catching their breath on a tiny snow ledge near the crest of the ridge. Petzoldt crawled around a rock outcropping to the end of the 60-foot rope that bound him to his partner. House heard a shout and followed. He found Petzoldt looking down on a 20-foot-wide shelf of snow, cradled against the side of the ridge.

It was big enough and flat enough to hold three tents—a perfect place to begin their assault on K2. "Instantly our attitude to the mountain changed," House recalled later. "With one campsite found we could find others."

4

How Small Indeed

The team started up the ridge on July 3. They attacked each segment of the climb with the same repeating rhythm. Two climbers went ahead to find the next campsite. The rest ferried loads of supplies up from the lower camps. While the supplies arrived, two more strapped on crampons and clawed out another foothold 1,000, maybe 1,500, feet higher.

Each segment had its own way of reminding them that no one had ever before set foot where they were climbing. To establish Camp III, Petzoldt and House had to carve steps into vicious ice slopes that dropped off more than 4,000 feet to the glacier beneath them. They put Petzoldt's pitons to work, hammering them into exposed rock wherever they could. When Houston followed, he had 900 feet of rope to keep him secured to the mountainside. To the amusement of his climbing partners, he was starting to lose the running debate with Petzoldt over climbing style. But

Bates using fixed ropes to guide him through a traverse between Camps II and III.

he still referred to the pitons scornfully as "ironware."

Camp III was a meager ledge with nothing to protect it from the elements. Kikuli and the rest of the Sherpas had to gather rocks and build a 4-foot wall to make a platform level enough for the tents. Even then, the climbers went to bed worried that if they rolled over in the night, they could launch themselves down the mountainside, wrapped in a tent.

On July 12, Houston and Petzoldt set off to carry supplies to Camp IV. As they dug for footholds, they discovered one of K2's most dangerous defenses. The slope was covered in loose rock. No matter how carefully they chose their route, they seemed to dislodge half the mountainside.

INTO THE CLOUDS

All day long, they sent a hail of rocks clattering down on their comrades in Camp III.

In the afternoon, Houston and Petzoldt climbed back into camp after dropping their loads at Camp IV. They offered up a cheery greeting and got nothing but cold stares in return. Three tents had been ripped and their inhabitants were shell-shocked from dodging rocks all morning.

It was a tense moment at 20,700 feet. Houston and Petzoldt had put in a day of hard work and got no thanks for it. The rest of the team felt their lives had been put in danger by their two careless teammates.

Houston and Petzoldt decided not to plead their case. Instead, they dug through the supplies and emerged with jam, dates, and hot tea for everyone. Before long, they were all laughing in the faded light, ready to take shelter in their newly ventilated tents and prepare to climb another day.

The next morning, though, Houston lay in his sleeping bag for what seemed like hours. All night he had dreamed of New Hampshire and New York. Now, he just wanted to be done with the mountain so he could get home and sleep in a warm bed. "Dreading days work and wishing job were done," he wrote. "Hated idea of going on."

▲

Above Camp IV lay the most treacherous terrain yet. Bates and House reached it on July 14—an 80-foot wall of rock, nearly vertical, with a single crack slanting up the length of the cliff. At sea level the cliff would have been challenging, even for an experienced climber. High on the face of K2, it looked nearly impossible. But there was no way around it. And if anyone could climb it, Bill House was the man.

Bates found an outcropping of rock at the base of the cliff and tied himself to it. Then he ran the rope that connected him to House around the rock to create friction. In the language climbers use to talk about their craft, this is what's known as a belay—a system of ropes and anchors that allows one climber to protect another from falling.

Bates's position was as good as he could make it. But as House climbed higher, the belay would give him less and less protection. If he slipped, he would fall twice the distance between himself and Bates before the rope went taut and stopped him from careening down to the glacier.

House began edging his way up the crack, finding tiny ridges in the rock face just big enough for fingers or the edge of a boot. He pressed hard against the sides for leverage.

About 20 feet up, the crack widened and he had to stretch too far for holds. So he wriggled into position with his back against one side of the crack and the soles of his boots wedged against the other side. Little by little he inched higher.

The crack narrowed, and House could again rely on tiny holds. It was grueling work, and he paused often to gasp for air. But the cliff gave him no real rest. Every second he spent clinging to the rock brought his forearms and shoulders that much closer to giving out.

About 40 feet above Bates, House found a ledge wide enough to take the pressure off his limbs. At this point, he was exhausted and close to his limit. If he fell from here, he would plunge 40 feet down the cliff and another 40 feet down a steep ice slope. The fall might not kill him. But it was unlikely he would escape without broken bones. This high on the mountain, he might as well be dead.

House pulled out a piton. He thought he saw a tiny crack big enough to pound the metal spike into. If he could secure it in the rock face, he could run his rope through the end to give him protection much higher on the cliff. But the piton dug a half inch into the rock and then crumpled like a weak nail.

He looked down at Bates, who hadn't been able to move since House started the climb. Bates was freezing, and he yelled up, hoping to convince House to come down. House wasn't sure how much strength he had left, but the climb down looked even more harrowing than what lay above him. He shouted a quick "no, thanks" and clawed his way upward.

Finally, he pulled himself over the lip of the cliff and lay panting at the top. It had taken him more than an hour to climb 80 feet. But his accomplishment would be talked about for decades to come. The cliff is one of the hardest

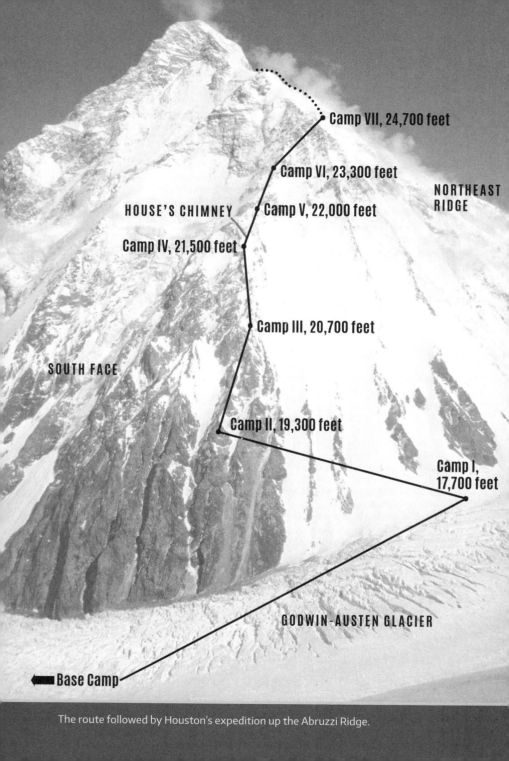

Camp VII, 24,700 feet

Camp VI, 23,300 feet

NORTHEAST RIDGE

HOUSE'S CHIMNEY

Camp V, 22,000 feet

Camp IV, 21,500 feet

Camp III, 20,700 feet

SOUTH FACE

Camp II, 19,300 feet

Camp I, 17,700 feet

Base Camp

GODWIN-AUSTEN GLACIER

The route followed by Houston's expedition up the Abruzzi Ridge.

climbs in high-altitude mountaineering, and he had done it with the only promise of protection coming from 80 feet below. That tiny crack high on the face of K2 would become known as House's Chimney.

▲

Three days later, everyone was safe in Camp V at the top of the chimney when a vicious storm rolled in. Houston didn't want to wait it out. On the mountain, he had a never-ending supply of cheerful, nervous energy. It seemed as though he never stopped moving.

Impatient to make progress, he and Petzoldt suited up the morning of July 17 and headed out to place the next camp. The wind hit them like a freight train. Their beards frosted over. Hands and feet went numb. In minutes they turned back for the shelter of the tents.

Kikuli greeted them with tea. "Just like Nanga Parbat," he said ominously.

The 1934 disaster on Nanga Parbat still haunted Kikuli. The German leaders of the expedition had made a furious push for the summit without taking time to stock the high camps with supplies. They made it to 24,500 feet before a raging blizzard shrouded the mountain. With no place to wait out the storm, 16 men had to fight their way down through blinding snow and winds strong enough to lift a 160-pound climber into the air.

Kikuli spent three nights exposed on the mountain

before stumbling to safety, snow-blind and frostbitten. Three German climbers and six Sherpas weren't so lucky. They froze or starved to death on the side of Nanga Parbat.

It was a story of bitter, prolonged agony, and every climber knew it well. Now, 22,000 feet up the slopes of K2, it was not a thought anyone wanted to dwell on.

In contrast to the German expedition, Houston had made sure every camp on K2 was well stocked. If this storm lasted, they could huddle at Camp V for ten days before they ran out of food.

But after five weeks on the mountain, the cold, the altitude, and the simple, relentless hardship was starting to take its toll. It had been months since they had slept on a mattress, sat at a table, or eaten a fresh vegetable. For two weeks, they hadn't stood on level ground. Put boots, cups, or bowls down carelessly and they went clattering into the abyss. Walk around unroped and inattentive and you could easily follow.

Everything required effort, and at times it seemed too much to bear. In the mornings they forced themselves out of their sleeping bags by letting the air out of their mattresses while they lay in the tent. When rocks poked them in the back, they got up and started the day.

A supply of mail had made it up from Base Camp on July 15. To House, the letters were almost too painful to read. He had gotten used to the frozen boots and damp socks, the frost on the tent melting onto his head every morning. He could stand it as long as he had nothing to compare it to. But the thought of everyone he loved going to sleep at night in soft beds and warm houses was enough to drive him crazy.

▲

By July 19, they had found a site for Camp VI, 23,300 feet up the Abruzzi Ridge. Once again, the Sherpas spent an afternoon hacking rocks out of the ice and stacking them in platforms to hold the tents. The nearest level ground lay 7,000 feet below. "We now felt further removed from the common world than ever before," Houston recalled. "Life at home, with its complications, petty annoyances, hopes and struggles, seemed futile and very, very far away."

Houston and Petzoldt had spent the day scaling the Black Pyramid, the complicated maze of steep rock and sheer ice that lay above Camp VI. By afternoon they had reached the top of the Abruzzi Ridge and found a site for Camp VII. Above them, a gradual snow slope led to the final 2,000-foot summit cone. Most of the Karakoram was laid out below—Broad Peak, Masherbrum, and the ominous Nanga Parbat. For Houston, the sight was exhilarating—like nothing else in the world. No human being had ever stood this high on K2.

Houston and Petzoldt hurried back to camp with a

decision to make. The team had ten days of food and fuel with them at Camp VI. If they decided to push for the summit, they would need at least one more camp and several more days. As long as the weather held, their supplies would last. But if a storm rolled in and trapped them high on the mountain, they would come perilously close to repeating the Nanga Parbat disaster.

The safe thing would have been to pack up and head down the mountain. Their goal had been accomplished. They had found a route up the second-highest peak in the world. Next year, Fritz Wiessner could follow their path to the top of K2. An American expedition would conquer the second-highest mountain on Earth, and they would have played a major role.

They talked for several hours—and decided to try for the summit.

▲

The next day, Houston and Petzoldt said goodbye to Bates, House, and Kikuli at the top of the Black Pyramid. The five men had lugged three days' worth of supplies more than 1,000 feet up from Camp VI. They had intended to leave all the Sherpas behind, but Kikuli begged to come at least this far. Houston and Petzoldt were still a treacherous ice traverse away from their campsite. But the others had to turn around to make it back to Camp VI by dark. They disappeared into the waning light, leaving Houston and

Houston makes the steep traverse to Camp VII with the Karakoram laid out behind him.

Petzoldt alone at 24,500 feet—the two highest men on Earth.

Despite their differences, the two climbers had become solid partners over the last 10 weeks. Now, they were joined by a 60-foot length of cord—the fellowship of the rope. They shouldered their supplies for the next three days and made their way across the ice slope. Protecting them from the abyss below were Petzoldt's pitons, driven deep into the mountainside.

They made it safely to Camp VII and set up a lone tent. They scooped snow into a pan to melt for drinking water and dinner. But when they went to light the stove, they rummaged in their packs and came up empty-handed. They realized in horror that they had left the matches at Camp VI.

Houston managed to find nine stray matches, loose in his pack. But there was no guarantee they would work. The first one fizzled out before it ignited the gas in the stove. The second broke off at the head when they tried to strike it. On the third try they finally got the stove to light.

It was absurd, really. A year of planning, five weeks of trekking, and five weeks of climbing had brought them within reach of the summit. And they had left something as essential as matches behind. It was such a simple mistake—like forgetting your wallet when you went out for groceries. But at 25,000 feet, you couldn't make a quick trip home. K2 didn't give second chances.

▲

The next day, July 21, Houston and Petzoldt went through three more matches at breakfast. Then they left to make their attempt at the summit. They each wore four wool sweaters, flannel shirts, and windproof suits, and still the cold bit through to their skin. To Houston it felt like ice water flowing through his bones.

Petzoldt led the way, obviously stronger. Before long they sank to their hips in fresh powder snow. Houston started to fall behind. He gasped at the thin air, trying to pull enough oxygen into his lungs—five, six breaths every step. He knew he was done, and the doubts overwhelmed him. What if he hadn't forgotten the matches and he had an extra day to rest? What if he had let Bates or House take his place? "I struggled on," he recalled later, "why I do not know, for it was foolish to try to gain a few more feet, and yet something within drove me to go as high as I possibly could."

When he finally stopped, he sat for a while. His medical training took over, and he took his own pulse. Even after a long rest, his heart still pounded out 135 beats per minute. At sea level, it would have been 50. They had made it above 26,000 feet with just a day's climb to go. And yet, Houston couldn't move another step higher.

Finally, Petzoldt stopped and began to work his way back to his partner. While Houston waited, a tiny speck on the broad back of the mountain, he was flooded with emotion. His entire life, he decided, had been leading to this one moment. He had come face-to-face with something infinitely larger than himself, and failed. The conditions couldn't have been better for a summit bid. Except for a few stormy days, the weather had been beautiful the entire time on the mountain. And yet, they had been so easily beaten. Nature had "let our puny bodies exhaust themselves in the rarefied atmosphere," he reflected later. "How small indeed we were to struggle so desperately to reach one point on the earth's surface."

That night, back at Camp VII, they went through their final three matches, trying to get the stove lit. The next day, without a warm breakfast, they started down the mountain to rejoin their friends and head for home.

PART TWO

1939
The Hermit
of K2

The Second American Karakoram Expedition
Standing from left: George Sheldon, Chappell Cranmer,
Jack Durrance, George Trench.
Seated from left: Tony (Eaton) Cromwell,
Fritz Wiessner, Dudley Wolfe.

5

Boys to Men

Eight months after he sat near the top of the world, pondering his place in the universe, Charlie Houston found himself at a dinner table on the wealthy Upper East Side of Manhattan. Sitting near him was a 26-year-old college student named Jack Durrance. The dinner was a final celebration for Durrance before he boarded a ship, crossed the Atlantic, and met up with Fritz Wiessner. Durrance was leaving to climb K2 with the Second American Karakoram Expedition. He would be following Houston's route up the mountain.

Houston was working in a New York hospital now, and the work left him little time to do anything else. But K2 was still on his mind.

He was worried about the expedition Durrance was about to join, and he couldn't resist letting the dinner guests know. Besides Wiessner, none of the climbers had much experience. Durrance had climbed some of the hardest rock walls in the western United States, but only Wiessner had been to the Himalaya before.

Durrance took the opportunity to ask Houston for some advice. He was just an undergraduate preparing for medical school, but there was no real doctor on the expedition. If anyone went down with altitude sickness or a broken limb, Durrance would have to treat him.

Houston gave the most practical advice he could: Watch out for frostbite. If anyone started showing signs, keep his toes or fingers clean and dry. Get him down the mountain quickly.

As dinner wore on, Houston tired of the talk about K2. Less than a year ago he had stood just 2,000 feet below the summit. He was convinced he had been right to turn back. His body had reached its limit. Without matches it would have been foolish to stay at the high camp and try again the next day. And publicly, Houston always said that the journey itself was more important than the goal.

But still, it was hard not to have doubts. The weather had been good. What if they had regrouped, resupplied the high camps, and tried again? Years later, Petzoldt insisted they should have done exactly that. "We made up our mind not to climb the mountain," he said. "If we'd have brought up a little bit more food and planned to get to the summit, we could have come back as conquerors of K2."

Could they have made it? Houston didn't know. But with

memories of K2 haunting him, he knew he didn't want to be at the dinner anymore. At 9:30 he got up, said his good-byes, and left abruptly. He spent the next couple of hours wandering the streets of New York, lost in thought.

▲

While Houston tried to come to terms with his memories of K2, Fritz Wiessner prepared his assault on the mountain. He was in Europe, stocking up on equipment and waiting for his team to assemble.

Thanks to Houston, Wiessner knew a lot more about the task ahead than he would have a year ago. Houston had drawn up a two-page, single-spaced description of his route up the Abruzzi Ridge. He described rock formations and ice climbs. He made corrections to the duke's map of the mountain from 1909. On the mountain itself, the team had left ropes and pitons in place to mark routes for Wiessner.

For all the tension that had built up between them, Houston and Wiessner had a lot in common. They had skied and climbed together. They were devoted to the mountains. And Wiessner shared Houston's desire to keep climbing simple. To him it was a test of skill and daring. A true mountaineer climbed with as little mechanical protection as possible and left the mountain in the same condition as he found it.

But as leaders, Houston and Wiessner couldn't have been more different. To Houston, every expedition was a democracy. When important decisions came up, he gathered his partners in a tent and took a vote. The fellowship of the rope came first, the summit second. Wiessner, on the other hand, had a reputation as a stubborn, single-minded leader. Once he chose a path, he stayed on it. He had little tolerance for people who couldn't—or wouldn't—keep up.

Unfortunately, among the climbers making their way to Europe to join the expedition, it was hard to pick out one who stood a chance of keeping up. That certainly wasn't the way Wiessner had planned it. He had tried to recruit the best mountaineers in the U.S., starting with Houston's team. He asked Bates, Burdsall, and House to join him. They all turned him down. House, for one, had climbed with Wiessner before. He knew how demanding his friend could be, and he had no desire to be stuck in the Himalaya with him for four months.

One by one, Wiessner's other top choices ruled themselves out. One couldn't afford the trip. Another dropped out when his wife had a miscarriage. A third broke his leg skiing just before the expedition left.

Wiessner was left with a makeshift team. He had three students from Dartmouth College—Durrance, George Sheldon, and Chap Cranmer. At 26, Durrance was by far the most experienced of the three. Sheldon had never been on a long expedition. Cranmer had climbed in Canada with Wiessner and in the Alps with his parents. But he hadn't ventured above 15,000 feet. He wasn't even old enough to vote.

The other two team members seemed to have been chosen more for their wealth than their climbing talents. Tony Cromwell was 47. He spent his days traveling in Europe, climbing the Alps with a guide. He told Wiessner before they left that he wouldn't climb above Camp IV.

The last team member was a sportsman named Dudley Wolfe. Wolfe was heir to a fortune dug out of the silver

Cromwell, Sheldon, and Cranmer with skis and ice axes, en route to K2.

mines of Colorado in the 1800s. He loved to ski and scale peaks in the Alps, but he had spent more time sailing yachts than climbing. He let his older brother manage the family businesses while he spent the proceeds on his adventures. At 42, Wolfe felt it was time to make his mark on the world, so he accepted Wiessner's invitation to climb K2.

In a letter, Wolfe assured his brother that he wouldn't take any unnecessary risks. Still, out of "good sense," he rewrote his will before he left.

▲

In Europe, the team spent ten days buying gear—gloves, boots, pitons, goggles, tents, and stoves. Before long, Wiessner ran out of money. At equipment shops and expensive restaurants, he handed the bills to Wolfe.

In mid-April, thanks in part to Wolfe's money, the climbers arrived in Srinagar with four tons of supplies. They were still a monthlong trek from the mountain, and Wolfe already felt uneasy about the team. Cranmer was so quiet it was nearly impossible to get to know him. Durrance and Sheldon seemed to treat the trip like a fraternity party. They got drunk on champagne and flirted with women. They started water fights and made fart jokes.

Wolfe began to wonder if they were truly prepared for K2. He had been urging Wiessner to buy two-way radios so they could communicate between camps on the mountain. Before they left Srinagar, he found out that Wiessner had ignored him. Wiessner hated technology, and in 1939, radio sets were bulky and heavy to carry. As a result, Wiessner had spent the money on other supplies. They would communicate by smoke signals, he said.

It was a ridiculous idea, Wolfe thought. Even if they had material to burn, the first puff of smoke would be blown into China on 50-mile-per-hour winds before it communicated anything to anyone.

▲

On May 2, despite his doubts, Wolfe joined a long line of porters and ponies loaded down with gear. The procession snaked out of Srinagar, following the same route Houston and his team had taken a year earlier. They made their way through desert plains, green apricot orchards, and narrow canyons flanked by high, crumbling cliffs.

Pasang Kikuli and a team of eight Sherpas had joined the men at Srinagar. A few of the men—Phinsoo, Pemba Kitar, and Sonam—had been with Kikuli the year before on Houston's expedition. On the trail, they set up tents for the sahibs, made them tea, and carried their personal gear. Kikuli was their *sirdar*, or leader. At this point, he was probably the most experienced Himalayan mountaineer alive. It would be his ninth expedition to the high peaks in 11 years. His feet were battered by frostbite from the disaster on Nanga Parbat, but he had come through Houston's expedition unhurt. Wiessner felt lucky to have him.

With ten days of trekking to go, Wolfe soaks his blistered feet in camp just past the village of Skardu.

Whatever hazards lay ahead, they didn't seem to worry Durrance and Sheldon. The two classmates bounded along the trail as though hiking were a competitive sport. They raced each other to the next ridge and played tag along the way. But as the route climbed toward the glacier that formed the final pathway to K2, they began to feel the elevation. Both Durrance and Sheldon were plagued by headaches and sleepless nights.

Wolfe took it all in without saying much. He wondered why Wiessner didn't step in and warn the boys to stop wasting their energy. As the days wore on, he tried to avoid the others. At night he aired out his blisters and massaged his throbbing ankles and shins. In the morning he left early or lagged behind.

INTO THE CLOUDS

As civilization receded, Wolfe wanted to get away from Wiessner's moods and the shrill laughter of the boys. They ruined the silent majesty of the land that welcomed them, day after day, into its sanctuary. By the middle of May they had put 200 miles between themselves and the nearest automobile. The last telegraph machine lay behind them in the town of Skardu. They were cut off from the outside world, jagged peaks towering overhead as they had for millions of years. Dudley Wolfe had never seen anything like it.

▲

On May 30, the climbers rounded a bend in the glacier and got their first glimpse of K2. They started up the Godwin-Austen Glacier, just ten miles from the base of the mountain. But as they counted off the final miles, the procession stalled. The porters, one after another, dropped to their knees in the snow. They clutched at their eyes and groaned in pain. They had been marching for days on the blinding white glacier without snow goggles to protect them. The sun's rays had seared the corneas of their eyes. They were going snow-blind.

It was a familiar story on Himalayan expeditions. The European or American climbers spent most of the money on their own gear. The porters were left to supply themselves. In the low valleys, temperatures could run over 100 degrees Fahrenheit. Most villagers wore sandals and thin wool shawls. They didn't have money to invest in heavy boots, jackets, or goggles. Expedition leaders simply picked the porters who looked best equipped and hoped they would last the entire journey.

So, as the 1939 expedition climbed into mountain weather, many of their porters trudged through the snow in torn sandals—even bare feet. At night, Wiessner, Wolfe, and the other Western climbers disappeared into tents and zipped themselves into down sleeping bags. The porters huddled together under tarps in the frigid wind. During the day, they faced the blinding glare of the sun without protection.

On the glacier, George Trench, the British transport officer who was in charge of the porters, tried to talk the group into moving. But the men refused. Snow blindness is intensely painful, and the only cure is to sit with a cold cloth on the eyes and wait for the swelling to go away. Finally, Durrance and Cranmer dug out some cardboard, cut it into strips, and carved slits for eye holes to filter the light.

With their makeshift sunglasses, most of the porters agreed to move on, but three of them still sat with their heads in their hands. From behind his store-bought snow goggles, Sheldon yelled at them: "Get up and get moving." But the men couldn't do it. Finally, they were paid off and sent home with help from two porters who could still see. With the five loads redistributed, the expedition turned toward the mountain for the final day's trek.

▲

Crossing the Braldu River in early May. At most river crossings, the porters took off their sandals and waded barefoot into the frigid water.

On May 31, a month after leaving Srinagar, the men stood at Base Camp surrounded by crates and bundles. They hadn't even begun to climb, and already they stood 2,000 feet higher than any piece of ground in the continental United States.

With the mountain looming above them, they began to have their private doubts. Sheldon wrote in his journal, "A trip like this, I believe, changes boys to men—they either come through or they don't, and if they don't it is too damn bad. But if they do, they'll be men. We shall see."

Durrance was convinced he would be the one who wouldn't come through. *I'm going to die on this mountain,* he thought as the men set up their tents and organized supplies. But before he could spend too much time imagining his own demise, he had another, more immediate crisis on his hands.

Their first morning in Base Camp, Cranmer woke with a raging fever. He shook uncontrollably and couldn't keep a morsel of food down. He was coughing up a frothy, green liquid, and Durrance could hear the fluid in his lungs every

Hours from Base Camp, Cranmer (left) and Sheldon get their first look at the summit.

time he took a raspy breath. Durrance thought it might be pneumonia. But, as he had told Houston, he wasn't qualified to be a doctor. He had no real idea what was wrong with Cranmer. He knew only that it sounded like his friend was dying.

6

The Siege

One after another, the soiled sleeping bags piled up outside the large Logan tent. Durrance had turned the tent into a hospital with Cranmer as its lone patient. Inside, he battled to keep his friend alive.

Cranmer groaned with pain from diarrhea and nausea. He couldn't keep anything down. He gasped and wheezed, trying to get oxygen past the thick fluid in his airways. Durrance pressed his mouth to Cranmer's and forced air into his lungs. He rocked his friend back and forth to keep the fluid from settling in one place. Delirious from fever, Cranmer babbled on about a baseball game he thought he was playing back at Dartmouth. At one point, he muttered that he had a one-in-three chance of surviving.

No amount of advice from Charlie Houston could have prepared Durrance for this. He hadn't set foot in a medical school classroom and he suddenly found himself in charge of someone's life. Wiessner and Cromwell had gone off

Cranmer's view for the rest of the expedition: looking south down the Godwin-Austen Glacier from Base Camp with the flat top of Chogolisa (25,100 feet) in the distance.

with Kikuli to scout their route up the mountain. Wolfe and Sheldon took turns caring for Cranmer in the hospital tent. But they relied on Durrance to figure out what to do.

Luckily for everyone, Cranmer began to improve. On the third day, his nurses lifted him out of the foul-smelling tent and propped him up in a camp chair in the sun. The patient would survive. But he was done climbing before he had started. Base Camp would be Cranmer's home for the rest of the mission.

When Wiessner got back from his scouting trek, he couldn't have been thrilled with the state of his expedition. He had been counting on Cranmer as one of his strongest climbers. Now, the young man who'd scrambled up some of

Canada's toughest peaks with Wiessner couldn't get up from a chair without help. Cromwell had already announced that he wouldn't be climbing past Camp IV. And Durrance, the most experienced mountaineer in the bunch, seemed exhausted already. At 17,000 feet, he was feeling the altitude, racked by headaches and sleeplessness.

And still, they had a mountain to climb.

▲

On June 5, Wiessner trudged out of Base Camp with a line of climbers behind him. They picked their way up the glacier, weighed down by tents and sleeping bags; shovels and coils of rope; food, stoves, and canisters of gas. The Sherpas carried 50 pounds each; the sahibs, 35.

The language of war is often used to describe what mountaineers do. Expeditions launch "assaults" on a mountain. Climbers "attack" a rock wall or a steep ice slope. An "army" of porters packs supplies to Base Camp. If the 1939 expedition was on a military mission, this was the beginning of the siege.

Like Houston the year before, Wiessner planned to establish a line of camps up the ridge with about 1,000 feet of climbing between each camp. Each step of the way, an advance party would press ahead and find a location barely level enough to keep a couple of tents from sliding off the mountainside. Along the route, they would place fixed ropes to help the rest of the expedition through the most exposed sections of the climb. The others would then ferry loads up from the camp below while two or three climbers went on to scout the next location.

Wiessner had one hard-and-fast rule: He wanted every camp fully stocked with food and sleeping bags. Rarely did K2 get more than four days of clear skies in a row. The weather had been kind to Houston the year before, but storms could easily roll in and trap climbers for days. Wiessner had known the German climbers who were forced into the deadly blizzard on Nanga Parbat in 1934. He wanted to make sure his own expedition could take shelter for as long as they needed in any camp.

On June 7, the team had spent three days in a row hauling loads up the glacier from Base Camp. They still had more than 10,000 feet of climbing to go. But already, the altitude made each load feel heavier than normal. At 17,000 feet, each breath gave them only half the oxygen they would get in New Hampshire or New York. At the end of the day, Durrance sank into his tent and picked up his diary. "There is no expression to describe how awful I felt physically today—" he confessed, "back ached—short winded and despondent spirits."

Two days later, Durrance was at it again, following Wiessner to Camp II. The route was steep, and Wiessner led the climb. For three hours, Durrance stood below him, paying out rope while Wiessner hacked steps into the ice

Durrance kicking steps into the slope, roped to a partner below.

and pounded pitons into cracks in the rock face. Durrance was still waiting on a pair of heavy-duty mountain boots he'd ordered from Switzerland. All he had were a pair of thin low-altitude climbing boots, and they made him feel like he didn't belong on the mountain. The traction was so poor he had to take extra care with every step. And the cold made the cheap leather feel like paper. Belaying Wiessner up the slope, he wiggled his toes constantly to keep frostbite from setting in.

Finally, by midday, they found the sheltered spot where Houston had set Camp II the year before. They dropped their loads and headed back to Camp I. Fumbling to get down in his inferior boots, Durrance watched while Wiessner scampered down the slope and disappeared below. Kikuli stayed behind to see Durrance back to camp. When they arrived, Wiessner was ready with an explanation. "I just wanted to see if you could take care of yourself," he said.

It seemed irresponsible for Wiessner to test him like that in the middle of a dangerous climb. But in the privacy of his own tent, Durrance wondered if Wiessner was right. The altitude sapped his energy. His boots ate away at his confidence. Maybe he wasn't up to the task.

At times, the mountain seemed to be threatening them with evil intent. Below Camp I, the glacier popped and groaned underfoot like a living being. The noise made everyone uneasy. Durrance was convinced the ground was about to yawn open under his tent and swallow him alive.

▲

A week later, the team still hadn't made it past Camp II, and Wiessner was beginning to feel that his suspicions were right: They couldn't get along without him. He didn't trust anyone but himself to lead the climbs. He would have to find the routes up the mountain, cut steps into the steepest ice slopes, anchor ropes to protect the climbers carrying loads. It was exhausting work, and it meant he would rarely be around to organize the supply trips from below.

He had left that job to Tony Cromwell. But Cromwell wasn't getting it done. A storm kept him trapped at Camp I one day. Another day he claimed the Sherpas didn't want to work. At 19,000 feet, there were plenty of reasons not to climb higher. Each morning it took every bit of willpower the men had to get out of bed. Moisture from their breath had settled on everything in the tents and frozen solid. Boots and sleeping bags had to be thawed. Snow had to be melted for tea. Outside, the wind howled and steep slopes of rock and ice loomed.

Tony Cromwell had plenty to complain about, and Dudley Wolfe was at the top of his list. On June 16, Wiessner was down in Base Camp, attending to some business. Cromwell, Durrance, and Wolfe roped up to descend from Camp II to I and bring a load back up. Wolfe struggled, especially on the way down. He measured every step as though it could be his last. By the end of the day, the slow pace of the climb was driving Cromwell crazy. Both he and Durrance lashed out at Wolfe. The yachtsman was a poor excuse for a mountaineer, they told him. He didn't belong on K2.

Wolfe defended himself. He was doing his share of the work, carrying just as much weight and climbing just as high. And he did it without complaining, which was more than he could say for the others, especially Durrance. If he was slow, that was only because he had respect for the mountain and its dangers.

When Durrance sat down to write in his diary that night, he expressed his doubts about Wolfe. Dudley was "sensitive" to criticism about his climbing technique, he wrote. "This trip & mountaineering is simply a bit more than he expected."

But after three weeks on the mountain, Wolfe was turning into the most reliable climber on the team, at least when he was pointed in the direction Wiessner cared about most: up. Before he left Base Camp for the serious push up the mountain, George Sheldon sent off a letter to the AAC summing up the team's progress. He put a positive spin on everything, neglecting to mention that Cranmer had almost died. When he got to Wolfe, he reported, "Dudley is up on the mountain and you can't get him to come down."

Weeks later, when those words reached New York, they would have a much different meaning than when they were written.

▲

On June 21, three ropes full of climbers picked their way up a steep rock face and stood on a narrow shelf of snow and loose rock. Underfoot was the nearly level rock platform of Camp IV, built by Houston's expedition the year before. The men dropped their 50-pound loads and stared up at a nearly vertical mass of dark granite, rising 150 to 400 feet high. Until now, K2 had given them a mix of snow fields and rock outcroppings. Here was the raw mountain— a castle wall separating the lower slopes from the lonely, wind-battered upper reaches of the Earth. The gate in the wall was a jagged, snow-filled crack carved vertically into the rock: House's Chimney.

Wiessner and the others congratulated themselves. They stood at 21,500 feet, almost a mile above Base Camp. The summit still stood nearly 7,000 feet above them. But they were finally making progress.

For Durrance, it hadn't been easy. His feet were freezing in his flimsy boots, and the climb from below had been harrowing. The lead climbers had tried to step carefully, but they couldn't help dislodging rocks. Dozens of feet down the slope, the rest of the team felt like they had stepped onto a battlefield. The bombs fell without much

Setting up Camp IV at the base of House's Chimney.

warning—a faint shout above the roar of the wind, maybe the clatter of stone on stone.

To Durrance it seemed like gambling. Clinging to the side of the mountain, there was little he could do to dodge the falling rocks. If one of them arrived with just the right speed and trajectory, it wouldn't matter how carefully he'd roped up, how expertly he chose his footholds. Nothing but luck stood between him and certain death.

Now, Durrance had survived the gauntlet. But as soon as he set down his load at Camp IV, he turned around to retrace his steps. His feet were on the verge of frostbite, and climbers were needed below to keep the chain of supplies moving up the mountain. He left with a team of Sherpas for the relative luxury of Camp II. There, he would meet up with Cromwell and start hauling loads back up to Camp IV while Wiessner pressed ahead.

Meanwhile, the advance party settled in near the base of House's Chimney. By dark, three tents stood on Charlie Houston's meager platform. Wiessner, Wolfe, and Sheldon climbed into one. Kikuli, Tse Tendrup, and Pasang Kitar bunked in another. The third sheltered their supplies.

They had just drifted off to sleep when the most terrifying storm Fritz Wiessner had ever seen shrieked in from the northwest and began to batter the slopes of K2.

▲

A couple of days into the storm, George Sheldon felt like he was losing his mind. He was trapped with Wiessner and Wolfe in a tent barely big enough for the three of them. Standing was impossible. To sit upright at the same time, all three men had to crowd into the center of the tent.

This was their prison. They left the shelter of the flimsy canvas only when they had no other choice—for bathroom breaks or to grab food and fuel from the supply tent. As soon they stepped outside, 80-mile-per-hour gusts threatened to launch them off the mountainside into Tibet. The air churned with particles of snow and ice—from the sky or the ground, it was impossible to tell. You could barely see your hand at the end of an outstretched arm.

The tents were hardly any comfort. The men huddled inside their sleeping bags, wrapped in several pairs of long underwear, wind suits, boots, and mittens. But the cold bit through every layer they had. The tent walls snapped and cracked under the force of the wind. The noise was deafening, and it never seemed to stop. Did they really think that a few yards of canvas could protect them from the raw power of the storm? All it would take was one tiny rip for the wind to tear their tent to shreds.

Sheldon was terrified. He had struggled to make it this high on the mountain. Like Wolfe, he was clumsy on the slopes. He looked to Wiessner for advice and comfort. And Wiessner—the great Fritz Wiessner—honestly seemed scared. In 27 years of climbing, he said, he had never seen a storm like this.

That was enough to send shivers of panic through George Sheldon's nervous system. That, and the

Sheldon: "My attitude about K2 is to get the hell out of here."

howling wind and the snapping of the tent and the sleepless nights he spent trying to massage feeling back into his frozen toes. He knew it was insane, but he had a terrible urge to rip open the door of the tent and run. Forget about his frostnipped feet, forget about the gale, forget about the fact that you couldn't see a thing outside. He just wanted to get off the mountain.

Two thousand feet below, in Camp II, Durrance and Cromwell wanted the same thing. For nearly a week, they had barely left their tents. Over the screaming of the wind, they read to each other. Mostly, they fantasized about leaving K2 behind. They planned detours for the trip home, savoring the options the way starving people dream of food. There would be a week of drinking in Srinagar, sightseeing in India, a little trekking for Durrance in the Dolomite mountains of Italy.

Mountaineers have a word for it when the desire to climb begins to disappear. They call it "crumping." It takes more than skill and fitness to scale the highest mountains on Earth. Climbers need something else to get them past frozen feet and fingers, headaches, nausea, sleepless nights, and days spent fighting 50-mile-per-hour winds. Maybe it's willpower, or the single-minded desire to stand on the summit. Maybe it's an addiction to the adrenaline that surges through the body when a single bad step could send you plummeting to your death.

Whatever that quality is, it can vanish at any time. And that is exactly what was happening to George Sheldon, Jack Durrance, and Tony Cromwell. Halfway up the second-highest mountain on Earth, they just wanted to go home.

▲

On June 29, the 13 climbers camped along K2's Abruzzi Ridge woke to an unfamiliar feeling. The mountain was silent for the first time in eight days.

At Camp IV, Wiessner and Wolfe emerged from their tents, filled with energy. Now, Wiessner felt, the mountain could be climbed. He and Wolfe would stay high. With the help of Pasang Kikuli, the most experienced climber in the Himalaya, they would force their way up the mountain. Finally, K2 would be theirs.

But for George Sheldon, the end of the storm could not have come too soon. He was desperate to get down the mountain. He stuffed his frozen feet into his boots and roped up with several of the Sherpas to descend.

As they disappeared over the lip of the overhang, Wiessner stood at the top yelling encouragement down the slope. To reach the summit, he needed help from below. He needed high camps stocked with food and sleeping bags. Sheldon would be fine, he thought, after a few days of recovery. Then he could rejoin them, hauling supplies up the mountain.

That was the last thing on Sheldon's mind as he climbed down toward Camp II. "My attitude about K2," he had written in his diary, "is to get the hell out of here."

7

Puppet Master

F ritz Wiessner could taste the summit. On the morning of July 1, he emerged at the top of House's Chimney, pounded a piton in, and ran ropes 80 feet down to Wolfe, Kikuli, and Tendrup. Soon they all stood at the top of the giant rock face, 22,000 feet above sea level. Here the wind blew harder and the slopes grew more exposed. The mountain felt wilder—even less like a place where humans belonged. And that was just as it should be.

Both Wiessner and Wolfe were feeling good as they set up Camp V. Wolfe's feet had suffered during their week-long imprisonment. But he was getting used to the altitude. Now that the storm had blown over, Wiessner figured Cromwell, Durrance, and the Sherpas were pushing supplies up the mountain. With fully stocked camps, they would be in great position to summit in the next week or two.

Two glaciers converge below Camp IV. At the top of House's Chimney, 500 feet above, Wiessner, Wolfe, and Tendrup looked down on the same view.

Later that day, two more Sherpas arrived with a note from below. Durrance had news: Camp II had survived the storm; Sheldon had made it down from IV, weak but safe; and best of all, Durrance's new boots had arrived with a bag full of mail! They were still hauling loads from Camp I to Camp II, Durrance wrote. Once they were done, they would start carrying up to IV, but he wanted to make sure that no one would be climbing above them and launch a bombardment of loose rock onto their heads. "Tony and I will remain in II until further orders from you," he wrote.

Wiessner was furious. Further orders?! Wasn't anyone down there capable of making decisions? He dashed off a note ordering them to stock the upper camps as soon as possible. "Dear Jack and Tony," the note began. "I am very disappointed in you."

When the message arrived in Camp II, it did not make Jack Durrance or Tony Cromwell eager to rope up, step into the wind and snow, and risk his life for Fritz Wiessner. In fact, just when Wiessner needed his exhausted support crew the most, he had managed to demoralize them even further. As another storm rolled in on July 2, Durrance took refuge in his tent and complained to his diary. "We move only as puppets," he wrote; "it is definitely a one man's trip."

▲

Three thousand feet above Camp II, the puppet master was on the move. After waiting out the storm for three days, Wiessner, Kikuli, and Tendrup hoisted 40-pound loads on their backs and got ready to climb. Wolfe stayed behind at Camp V to receive supplies from below and send the loads up in Wiessner's wake.

It was slow going in fresh snow for the climbers. Wiessner, who had led nearly the entire way up the mountain, once again broke trail. He sank deep with every step, laboring to breathe in the thin air.

Finally, they found the four tent platforms of Camp VI, carved into the mountainside the year before by Houston and his team. They dropped their packs and pitched a tent, clinging to a steep slope with a tall rock buttress rising above them.

The next morning they scrambled through the treacherous rock slopes of the Black Pyramid. It was some of the most frightening climbing on the mountain—relentlessly steep and exposed. Wiessner placed pitons where he could and strung fixed ropes to help the team through the maze of rock and ice.

A day later, Wiessner had seen no sign of supplies from below. Had his note had no effect at all on the group at Camp II? What were they doing down there? He followed his tracks back to Camp V and found Wolfe completely alone and running low on supplies. Always awkward climbing down, Wolfe had been afraid to descend. But each day he had gone to the top of House's Chimney and yelled down the cliffside, hoping to see Durrance and Cromwell leading a caravan of Sherpas up from below. Instead, there was only the howling wind and the stunning view of the glacier a mile down the mountain.

Wiessner stormed down the mountain to get the supply train moving again. When he appeared out of the blowing snow on the afternoon of July 9, the miserable residents of Camp II hadn't seen their leader in nearly three weeks. "Lo and behold, Fritz came forth from the hanging fogs of K2 alone yesterday aft," Durrance wrote. "It was about 3:30 p.m. when he appeared looking somewhat worn since I saw him last 18 days ago."

Leading a climb to 25,000 feet was enough to make anyone look worn, but Wiessner was in good shape compared to his companions. Sheldon's feet had only gotten worse. He had retreated to Base Camp, and no one expected to see him on the mountain again. Durrance, Cromwell, and the Sherpas had gotten two loads halfway to Camp IV. But Cromwell had taken a bad fall and limped back to camp with a dull ache in his ribs. He was already planning their retreat. He had sent a note to Askole, the nearest village, ordering the porters to be at Base Camp by July 23, ready to haul their supplies out.

Wiessner was livid with Cromwell for organizing the porters. He was in no mood to retreat, and he told them all in no uncertain terms. Two days ago he had powered his way to the top of the Abruzzi Ridge, 3,000 feet from the summit of K2. Not a single human being had ever stood at the top of an 8,000-meter peak, and they had a chance to be the first. But in order to do it, he needed support from below. Now that Durrance had his new boots, Wiessner was counting on him to be part of the summit team. As for Cromwell, his job was to rouse the Sherpas and get them to stock the high camps.

Wiessner's speech got the team moving again, but it was a reluctant crew that dragged themselves out of their tents the next morning and prepared loads to carry up the mountain. Cromwell was sullen. They hadn't seen Wiessner in two and a half weeks, and now he appeared in camp demanding that they climb? And why was he so upset that they had summoned the porters for July 23? Wiessner had agreed to that plan weeks ago. It didn't mean the advance party had to be ready to leave then. They merely had to get most of the gear to Base Camp to be hauled off the mountain.

As for Durrance, for the first time in weeks he felt motivated to climb. But the summit? He was already racked by headaches and sleepless nights at 19,000 feet. How could he drag himself 9,000 feet higher?

On July 11, Durrance swallowed his doubts and set out for Camp V with Wiessner, Cromwell, and a team of Sherpas. Before they shouldered loads for the final push up the mountain, he sat down to describe the state of the expedition in his diary. "Pop Sahib [Cromwell] declares he is now used up and no good above IV," he wrote. "George Sheldon is an invalid with frostbitten toes in Base Camp, Chap Cranmer still too weak to visit I and II so that Fritz, Dud & I are the only ones left."

▲

On the morning of July 12, Durrance tied a rope around his waist and wedged himself into House's Chimney. With help from above, he found what meager footholds he could and worked his way up. When he pulled himself over the final ledge, there was Dudley Wolfe, greeting him like he had just walked in the doorway of Wolfe's home.

Except for a brief visit from Wiessner, Kikuli, and Tendrup, Wolfe had been alone at Camp V for a week. A

Hauling loads through the loose rock toward House's Chimney.

week with nothing to break the monotony but meals— oatmeal or cream of wheat? tea or broth?—and daily trips to the top of House's Chimney to search for signs of movement from below. In his diary, Durrance gave Wolfe a new nickname: The Hermit of K2.

As the rest of the team made its way up from IV, laden with supplies, Wolfe welcomed Durrance into his tent at Camp V and handed him a cup of broth. Then he asked for a quick medical exam. When Wolfe wrestled the boots off his swollen feet, Durrance did not like what he saw. One of Wolfe's feet was blistered with the beginnings of frostbite. Remembering Charlie Houston's advice, Durrance told Wolfe he should congratulate himself on a climb well done, say goodbye to Wiessner, and get himself down the mountain. At a lower altitude, his circulation would improve and his feet would thaw. If he stayed high, he could easily end up losing toes.

Wolfe wouldn't hear it. Aside from the feet, he was feeling strong. And after what seemed like a lifetime of waiting, the rest of the expedition had caught up to him. They had 10 climbers standing on the top half of the mountain. Wiessner was convinced they were going to conquer K2, and he was counting on Wolfe for the summit push.

By late morning, Cromwell was headed down to Base Camp. Durrance, Wolfe, Lama, Kikuli, Dawa, Tendrup, Pasang Kitar, Tsering, and Phinsoo all shouldered loads and followed Wiessner up the wind-whipped snow slope toward Camp VI. Finally, supplies were moving up the mountain.

For Durrance, the climb was harrowing. He brought up the rear, spent from yesterday's work. Wolfe and two Sherpas climbed ahead of him on the rope. They picked their way up steps kicked into the snow by Wiessner. The route wasn't hard, but it was steep, and without much exposed rock, Wiessner hadn't been able to place fixed ropes. They had only each other for protection.

Ahead of Durrance, Wolfe wobbled along on his frost-nipped feet. He looked strong, but unstable. Durrance watched in horror as he stumbled and nearly lost his balance, then stumbled again. If Wolfe slipped, his weight would pull all four of them into free fall. Durrance could jam his ice axe into the snow and hope for the best. But he could barely haul himself up the slope. He didn't have the strength to stop 500 pounds of weight from hurtling down the mountain to the glacier.

When they finally stumbled into Camp VI, Durrance crawled into a tent with Wolfe. He had climbed 4,000 feet in two days, and his body wasn't adjusting to the altitude change. Every part of him yearned for oxygen. He felt like a giant pile of rocks lay on his chest.

Somehow, Durrance summoned the energy to light into Wolfe. Wolfe had no business climbing higher, Durrance insisted. He had nearly pulled them off the mountain

Kikuli on the steep slopes at Camp VI.

several times today. And Wolfe was even more dangerous on the descents. He couldn't get down the mountain without help from others, and at this altitude a climber shouldn't be dependent on anyone else.

Wolfe listened to the lecture but couldn't help feeling annoyed. He had been high on the mountain for weeks and ready to climb higher. It was Durrance and Cromwell who had been holding up the expedition. Wolfe thought Durrance was just jealous, but he went to Wiessner to make sure the expedition leader hadn't lost confidence in him. Wiessner reassured him that he was doing fine. If at any point the climbing got too hard, Wolfe could stay back "in reserve."

Wiessner's reaction added to a suspicion Durrance had been harboring for weeks. Wiessner and Wolfe, Durrance thought, had an unspoken arrangement. In exchange for Wolfe's money, Wiessner was going to get him to the top of K2. "It is unfair to take a man along and use valuable time hauling him about just because he was able to finance the undertaking," Durrance wrote, "and also dangerous if conditions hit him just right when he is dependent on his own resources."

▲

The next day, however, on the way to Camp VII, it was Durrance who couldn't take care of himself. Just 100 feet into the climb, the treacherous Black Pyramid loomed above. Durrance felt panic rise into his chest. No matter how much air he sucked into his lungs, it wasn't enough. His head swam. He felt like he was suffocating in the open air.

Finally, he sat in a heap in the snow and called ahead for Wiessner. They agreed Durrance would turn around and go back to Camp VI with Kikuli, Dawa, Tsering, and Phinsoo. If he didn't feel well enough to climb the next day, he could stay there and direct the movement of supplies to the highest camps.

Durrance clung to the rope on the way down. When they made it to camp, he collapsed in the tent, his lungs still heaving. His heart beat wildly, trying to pump oxygen-starved blood to his organs. He was so frightened that he made Dawa sleep next to him to keep track of his breathing.

The next day, Durrance woke the Sherpas at 5:30. He was desperate to get down the mountain and needed their help. He ordered Phinsoo and Tsering to stay high and carry more supplies up to Wiessner. Kikuli's frostbite had returned and he was on the verge of losing his toes. He and Dawa roped up with Durrance and dragged him down the mountain to Camp II.

Jack Durrance was done with K2.

8

A Perfect Day to Summit

The night of July 14, a storm rolled in and shrouded the mountain. The wind whipped long swirling tails of snow from the summit. Falling snow blanketed the tents in four tiny outposts, strung along the mountainside and separated by thousands of feet of elevation. There, in varying states of deterioration, the remnants of Wiessner's team waited out the storm. They had arrived together at the end of May. In six weeks, K2 had torn them apart.

At the top of this broken chain of climbers stood Wiessner, Wolfe, and Pasang Lama. They had pitched a tent on a broad shoulder of snow at 25,300 feet: Camp VIII. They were the highest men on Earth, and Wiessner was primed to go higher. He had supplies for several days, and he thought Durrance was recovering in Camp VI, directing five Sherpas to bring more. He had either ignored the signs that his expedition was crumbling below him or decided he didn't care. He was determined to push for the summit.

Down the mountain, the rest of the team simply wanted to go home.

At Base Camp, Cromwell, Sheldon, and Cranmer counted the days until the porters arrived. Above them in Camp II, Durrance tried to recover his strength while Kikuli nursed his frozen feet.

Another 4,000 feet up the mountain, Tendrup, Tsering, Pasang Kitar, and Phinsoo huddled in the cramped tents of Camp VI. They had orders to carry more loads to the camps above them. But to get there, they had to negotiate the steep, broken rock of the Black Pyramid and the treacherous ice slope below Camp VIII. The Sherpas were climbing in boots similar to the ones Durrance had complained about during his first weeks on the mountain. They had no crampons and no Fritz Wiessner to carve steps for them. Without a better-equipped lead climber, they did not want to move.

▲

On July 17, Wiessner woke to clear skies and a light wind at Camp VIII. There was no sign of Durrance or the Sherpas. Kikuli, who he had hoped would be with him near the top, hadn't returned. And Wolfe was finally showing signs of wear. But the summit stood just 3,000 feet overhead. Two days of climbing and Wiessner could be the first man to stand astride one of the coveted 8,000-meter peaks. Pasang Lama had been climbing as well as anyone on the mountain. Wiessner decided to make do with the climbing party he had.

Wiessner and Pasang Lama's high point, 27,500 feet

Camp IX, 26,050 feet

Camp VIII, 25,300 feet

Camp VII, 24,500 feet:
Wolfe's final camp

Wiessner and Pasang Lama's route to the summit.

That morning, Wiessner, Wolfe, and Lama roped up and slogged up the slope through soft, fresh snow. After a couple hours of extreme effort, they stood at the lip of a crevasse, a long crack in the ice field that blocked their way to the summit cone. Crevasses are a sneaky hazard for high-altitude climbers. They often fill with snow from storms or avalanches. The snow offers a tempting bridge across the crevasse, but each step is a gamble. No one knows what lies below—an awkward 6-foot drop and a scramble back to the top, or a 100-foot plunge into darkness.

With Lama anchoring him at the edge of the crevasse, Wiessner stepped onto the snow bridge. He sunk immediately to his hips. As carefully as he could, he waded through the snow. When he finally hauled himself over the lip of the crevasse, he dug a firm belay position into the slope and helped Lama across. The two men now turned to encourage Dudley Wolfe.

Wolfe plunged into Wiessner's tracks, but every step was a struggle. He felt like he was swimming in quicksand and sinking deeper with every movement. He could probably keep fighting, but suppose he made it to the other side? The climbing would only get harder, the air thinner. Through sheer force of will he had outlasted everyone on the expedition except Pasang Lama and the great Fritz Wiessner. Now, he had finally reached the end of his strength.

"It's hopeless, Fritz," he called across the crevasse. "I just can't make it."

Wolfe fought his way back out of the crevasse. He told Wiessner he would go back to Camp VIII and recover. When Tendrup and Pasang Kitar arrived with supplies, maybe he would try again.

He reached to his waist and untied the rope that bound him to Lama and Wiessner. He let the rope drop, located the tracks they had made on the way out of camp, and headed down the mountain.

One by one, the members of the Second American Karakoram Expedition had dropped away. The team had failed to give Wiessner the support he wanted. Pasang Lama was not the partner he had expected to be left with at this point in the climb. And yet, here they stood, 3,000 vertical feet from the top of K2. One more camp and the summit would lie within reach.

This was the moment Wiessner had been fighting for. The weather looked promising. Most of the mountain lay below them. Wiessner and Pasang Lama turned toward the summit of K2 and climbed.

▲

A mile and a half down the mountain, Jack Durrance was lounging in the sun at Camp II when Dawa bounded into view with a note from Cromwell at Base Camp. The porters were arriving in less than a week, and Cromwell was collecting gear for them to haul off the mountain. He wanted Durrance to strip the lower camps and bring loads down with him. "Salvage all the tents & sleeping bags you can," the note said.

Durrance grumbled about the order to his diary. "Easier said than done!" he wrote. After three days of rest, he felt like he had rejoined the world of the living. But that didn't mean he was ready to haul 50-pound loads around at 19,000 feet. He had lost nearly 30 pounds since he left New Hampshire. In the Rockies, below 15,000 feet, he could cope with exhaustion. He could use every ounce of his strength one day, get a good night's sleep, then get up and do it again. In the Himalaya, it didn't work that way. On K2, you never recovered.

Kikuli was still in danger of losing his toes to frostbite, but he had been feeling torn between his own safety and his duties as head Sherpa. He agreed to take Dawa, climb the loose rock slopes to IV, and strip the camp. They returned with 70-pound loads of sleeping bags, tents, and other supplies. The next day, Durrance roused himself enough to join them. The three men trudged down to Base Camp, burdened with supplies.

Besides complaining about the effort it required, Durrance did not question the order from Cromwell. Both of them knew that the high camps were still well supplied. And when the summit party came through, they would

Camp II, carved into the side of K2 at 19,300 feet.

probably have their own sleeping bags. From below House's Chimney they should be able to make Base Camp in a day.

Still, it had been Wiessner's plan to make sure all camps were stocked. They had expended a tremendous amount of effort hauling loads up the Abruzzi Ridge. The five camps above them had taken more than five weeks to supply. Now, the mountain lay nearly empty for 7,000 feet above Base Camp.

▲

On July 19, when Fritz Wiessner emerged from his tent at Camp IX, he had no idea what was happening on the mountain below him. He knew only that the skies were clear and the wind calm. It was a perfect day to summit K2.

At 9:00 a.m., he and Pasang Lama shouldered light loads and got under way. It was a late start for a summit push, and some of the hardest climbing on the mountain lay ahead.

Before long, they stopped to catch their breath. They leaned on their ice axes and stared up at K2's last obstacle— a giant overhanging cliff of snow and ice, called a serac, which guards the final climb to the top.

From below, Wiessner could see two possible routes, and neither looked good. Just beneath the serac lay a narrow corridor of ice, as steep as anything they'd climbed. If they chose that route, they'd have to carve steps upward and to the left in the shadow of the overhang. There were few places to anchor a rope. If one of them slipped, the other would be helpless to stop the fall. For 300 feet, they would have to move at a snail's pace with several tons of ice hanging over their heads. At any moment, a stray chunk could give way to gravity, break loose, and sweep them off the slope.

The second route lay farther to the left, out of reach of the serac. But it posed another challenge. Between the two climbers and the easy snow slopes of the summit stood a couple hundred vertical feet of steep rock, glazed with ice. At sea level, the climb would demand great strength and skill. At 27,000 feet, it was nearly impossible. Most climbers would have rejected the route immediately.

Fritz Wiessner was not like most climbers.

Always more comfortable on rock than ice, Wiessner chose the second route. He removed his crampons to get a better purchase on the rock. Then, for nine hours, he led Lama through some of the most difficult high-altitude climbing anyone has ever attempted. Risking frostbite, he took off his gloves so he could feel the rock beneath his fingers. He powered his way up an icy overhang. For two more rope lengths, he worked the rock face while Lama belayed him from below. When the rope went taut, he anchored himself with a piton, wrapped the rope around his hips and helped Lama up the route.

At around 6:00 p.m., Wiessner clung to the rock just below the top of the cliff face. One more 25-foot traverse,

Pasang Lama, anchored into the mountainside at 27,000 feet during his push toward the summit with Wiessner.

and he would pull himself onto the gradual snow slopes that led to the summit. From there, it was just a three- or four-hour slog through the snow to the top of K2. Finally, the goal he'd been dreaming about for years lay within his grasp.

But as he started the traverse, Wiessner felt the rope go taut around his waist. He looked down and saw Pasang Lama glaring up at him, shaking his head. Night was not far off, and the Sherpa did not want to be stuck high on the mountain in the pitch-dark. He was refusing to move.

Fritz stared down the rock face in disbelief. He had just made the most spectacular effort of his climbing career. It had brought them closer than anyone had ever been to the top of an 8,000-meter peak. Just 60 more feet of technical climbing, and they would stroll to the top. He tried to tell Lama that the worst was behind them. He explained that they were a long way from the safety of Camp IX. No matter what they did, they would be climbing in the dark. It would be better to take their time climbing to the summit and then descend the rock face in the light of the morning.

Lama simply held the rope tight and refused to budge. "Tomorrow," he said.

For seven weeks, Pasang Lama had climbed step for step with Fritz Wiessner. He had outlasted Kikuli and every other Western climber on the expedition. But he was not going to challenge the highest reaches of K2 in the middle of the night.

For Wiessner, it was a moment of great tension. He could have dropped the rope and tried for the summit on his own, leaving Lama to fend for himself. After all, he was a simple three-hour climb from a final step that would change his life. "If we get up," he had barked during one of Durrance's pouts, "we shall all be the most famous alpinists in the world!"

Instead, Fritz Wiessner decided it would be too dangerous for his partner to climb down alone. He told Lama to belay him. He turned his eyes away from the top of K2 and started the treacherous descent to Camp IX.

▲

The next day, July 20, the four Sherpas at Camp VI woke to bright blue skies and a calm wind. Outside their tents, the mountain glistened under the blinding sun. It was a beautiful day on K2—and no one was in a mood to enjoy it.

Tendrup and Pasang Kitar had last seen Wiessner on July 14. They had climbed with him to Camp VIII, dumped their loads, and descended to join Tsering and Phinsoo. Since then, the four men had been stuck in limbo. Wiessner expected them to carry more supplies to VIII, but the climbing was treacherous, and they weren't equipped to face it.

And so they waited—in conditions that grew more

unbearable by the day. Their tents rested on tiny platforms, carved into a slope as steep as a roof. Outside the tent flaps, they could take two steps on level ground. If they wanted more exercise, they had to dig steps into the slope and climb. Meanwhile, the altitude ate away at their health. Tendrup and Pasang Kitar had been above 20,000 feet for a month, Phinsoo and Tsering for the better part of three weeks. They were losing weight. Every day, their bodies grew weaker.

What were their choices? Climbing was their livelihood. If they ignored orders and descended, word could get around that they were unreliable. But if they attempted the ice slopes alone to bring supplies or check on the summit team, they might not live to climb again. Wiessner, Wolfe, and Pasang Lama had been high on the mountain for six days. How long did they need to make the summit? How long could they even survive at that great height?

Finally, Tendrup decided he had to do something. In the glare of the sun, he roped up with Pasang Kitar and Phinsoo and led the way up the Black Pyramid. Leaving his partners at Camp VII, he made his way cautiously up the ice slope above the Pyramid. He had no crampons to grip the ice and no one to belay him. After a while he stopped, unwilling to go farther. He balanced on the slope and peered up the mountain. Camp VIII couldn't have been more than 500 vertical feet above him. Between his perch and the camp, he thought he saw signs that an avalanche had swept the slope clean.

Tendrup tilted his head and yelled up the mountainside. There was no reply.

He yelled again. With a gentle wind, the mountain was quiet. Sound traveled far.

Still he heard nothing.

He tried one more time. Then he turned, gathered Pasang Kitar and Phinsoo, and climbed down the Black Pyramid to Tsering. There was no sign of the summit climbers, he told them all. As far as he could tell, Wiessner, Wolfe, and Pasang Lama had been swept off the mountain by an avalanche.

9

Deserted

At the top of the ice slope that had terrified Tendrup, Dudley Wolfe was very much alive—if not exactly well. On the morning of July 22, two days after Tendrup's calls had failed to rouse him, Wolfe drowsed in his tent at Camp VIII. It had been five days since he said goodbye to Wiessner and Pasang Lama at the lip of the crevasse. Once again, the Hermit of K2 had been alone on the mountain for nearly a week, this time at 25,300 feet.

Wolfe was fast running out of supplies. He'd never been good at lighting camp stoves and had burned through his supply of matches. Luckily, the weather had been beautiful. He'd been able to collect snow on a tarp, let it melt in the sun, and soothe his raspy throat with sips of clear, cold water. Still, he'd been living on canned ham, pemmican, cheese, and crackers. He was losing weight fast. For weeks, his brain had been starved for oxygen. It took a long time now to do simple tasks. He wasn't thinking clearly or quickly.

As daylight gradually warmed the air in the tent, he heard the sound of boots crunching in the snow. Then a voice came through the tent flap. With effort, he pulled himself into a crouch and crawled out the door. He stood awkwardly on his frostbitten feet and greeted his two visitors from the upper reaches of K2: Fritz Wiessner and Pasang Lama.

Wiessner took in the condition of the camp and its lone resident. He was enraged. He and Lama and even Wolfe were driving their bodies to the edge of collapse on the highest reaches of the mountain. And they were getting no support from below. The entire expedition seemed to have fallen apart while he was not around to supervise. Where were the Sherpas who had promised to bring supplies from below? Where was Jack Durrance? Didn't they understand he could not climb K2 alone?

When he calmed down, Wiessner filled Wolfe in on the summit attempt. After darkness cut their first attempt short, Wiessner and Lama had taken a rest day and then tried the ice slope directly under the serac. It was no use. On their nighttime descent from the rock face, Lama had gotten his pack tangled in the ropes. As he wrestled it free, their crampons came loose and clattered down the mountainside. Without them, the ice traverse was treacherous and slow. They didn't have the strength or the daylight to finish the climb.

Wiessner hadn't given up on the summit. In fact, he had left his sleeping bag at Camp IX. He'd been hoping to find fresh supplies and a rested climbing partner at Camp VIII and head back up the mountain.

That was now out of the question. They would have to descend, at least for now.

▲

Once again, Dudley Wolfe found himself in his least favorite position on the mountain—pointed down. Wiessner led the way through a thick fog, kicking steps in the snow and ice for the others to follow. Slowly they made their way down the same treacherous slope that had turned Tendrup back two days earlier.

A few hundred feet above Camp VII, they lost their precarious hold on the mountain. Wolfe got tangled in the rope and pulled Wiessner off-balance. Wiessner started to slide down the slope, scraping at the snow with his ice axe to slow his fall. But before he could bring himself to a stop, the rope went taut and yanked Wolfe and Pasang Lama off the slope. They careened down past Wiessner, jerking him into a somersault as they fell.

The three men tumbled down the slope, headed for a rim that dropped off into cliffs of rock and ice. If they went over the edge, there would be nothing to stop them but the glacier, 7,000 feet below. As they slid ever closer to the rim, Wiessner could feel the snow soften under him. He had a

Climbing fixed ropes above Camp II.

good grip on the axe now. He thrust it deep into the snow and held on with all his strength. The rope bit into his waist as Lama and Wolfe began to slow. Lama would later say that the rope caught on a rock. But whatever the cause, Wiessner felt himself come to a stop, facedown in the snow.

The tension on the rope eased. Below Wiessner, Dudley Wolfe and Pasang Lama had also stopped falling. They clung to the slope, not more than 60 feet above the edge of the cliff.

The men picked themselves up and staggered into Camp VII just before dark. Wolfe had lost his pack and his sleeping bag with it. Pasang Lama had been battered in the fall. He had broken a rib, and his lower back felt like it had been beaten with a sledgehammer. But as Wiessner looked around, he realized they had bigger problems.

He could barely believe his eyes. The camp looked like it had been ransacked by wolves. Two tents remained, but one of them had collapsed, its poles bent and broken. The other had been buried in snow. Food lay scattered on the ground along with two stoves and some fuel. There were no sleeping bags to be found.

While they cleared snow off the one working tent, Wiessner used what strength he had left to rage at the men below. Not only had they left their leader and two others to fend for themselves high on the mountain, they had stolen supplies that were essential for survival. If he and Wolfe ever made it back alive, they should have the others charged with criminal negligence!

"It was obvious to us that nobody had been at VII for many days or cared about the 3 men above," Wiessner wrote in his diary. "To the hell with them!"

Wiessner was still fuming as they zipped themselves into the tent. The temperature plummeted. The three men huddled together with nothing but a thin Sherpa sleeping bag to cover them, hoping they would survive the night.

▲

The fog that had blanketed the ice slope during the summit team's near-fatal plunge hung over Base Camp the next day. In the afternoon, Cromwell and Durrance were busy organizing gear for the porters when four weary Sherpas appeared out of the mist. They laid down a heavy load of sleeping bags, stoves, and other gear. Then Tendrup told their story.

The Sherpas felt terrible about descending from Camp VI before they made contact with Wiessner and Wolfe. Tendrup insisted he had gone as high as he dared and heard no sign of life from above. The slopes near Camp VIII had been swept by avalanches, and it was doubtful the summit team had escaped. He knew the porters were coming soon, and the sahibs would not want to leave valuable gear on the mountain. With no one to advise them, he and the other Sherpas did what they thought was right. They stripped Camps VII and VI and got down the mountain in time for the porters to haul the gear out.

Tendrup's story fueled the worst fears of the Base Camp party. They had already started to worry about the advance team. After all, Wiessner had reached Camp VIII on July 14, nearly 10 days before. From there, the summit shouldn't have been more than a three-day round trip. Except for two days of storm, K2 had given them perfect climbing weather.

As soon as Tendrup finished, Durrance and Cromwell went to the edge of camp and scanned the mountain with binoculars. They could barely see a thing through the fog. The next day, they decided, Cromwell would take Kikuli and Dawa up the glacier to look for signs of life on the ridge.

▲

Earlier that morning, as Tendrup moved down the mountain with news of their deaths, the three climbers at Camp VII were feeling relieved to be alive. They had sat upright in the darkness for hours, clutching Pasang Lama's sleeping bag to their chests. No one slept for more than minutes at a time.

It had been the most miserable night of Fritz Wiessner's life. He was about to follow it with the worst decision he would ever make.

As the sun rose and warmed the air on July 23, only two of the three men at Camp VII—Wiessner and Pasang Lama—prepared to descend. Wiessner would say later that he was simply going to Camp VI to find supplies for another summit bid. Wolfe wanted to summit with him and insisted on waiting at Camp VII.

But could either of them really have believed that the summit of the second-highest mountain on Earth was still within reach? All three men at this point had spent more time above 25,000 feet than anyone thought was possible. And the ordeal on the ice slope the day before had brought them to the brink of exhaustion. In addition to cracking his ribs, Lama had damaged his kidneys. He was peeing blood. Even if Wiessner had the strength to keep climbing, was he really going to leave the injured Sherpa to get down the mountain by himself?

Wolfe may have been in even worse shape than Pasang Lama. He had reached his limit a week before in the deep snow above Camp VIII. Since then, he'd been wallowing in the Death Zone without enough water or food. Could an experienced mountaineer like Wiessner have thought he was going to drag Wolfe to the summit of K2?

Or was there another reason to leave Wolfe by himself at 24,700 feet? Wolfe could have sensed he was too big a burden and stayed to avoid endangering the others. Wiessner might have known he couldn't get Wolfe down the mountain without help from below.

Whatever ran through the oxygen-deprived brains of the men at Camp VII, by late morning, Wiessner and Lama stood at the edge of camp, roped together and ready to descend. They had found a box of matches at the camp. Wiessner left Wolfe with 15 of them and took the rest for himself. As he and Pasang Lama made their way down toward the Black Pyramid, Wiessner saw several more matches strewn in the snow. He called back to Wolfe, telling him to collect them and dry them out. He might need them.

Then Wiessner and Pasang Lama descended the slope, and Dudley Wolfe disappeared from view.

10

The Most Beautiful Monument

On July 24, Cromwell, Kikuli, and Dawa were roaming the glacier below Camp I, scanning the mountainside for signs of life, when two walking skeletons appeared in the distance. The two climbers moved fitfully, falling to their knees on the snow and rocks every few steps. Cromwell hurried toward them until it was clear: Wiessner and Pasang Lama had made it down the mountain.

"Thank God you're alive!" Cromwell exclaimed.

Wiessner glared at him and spit out some vicious words. His voice was hoarse, and he could barely stand, much less climb. But no amount of exhaustion could mask his anger. The men stumbled back into Base Camp. Then Wiessner exploded.

In a raspy whisper, he railed at Cromwell, Durrance, and the Sherpas. Cromwell had been his second-in-command, and he had put the entire expedition at risk. What could possibly be his excuse for stripping the camps? And why did Tendrup, Tsering, and the others ignore the order to bring supplies to the higher camps? He could have Tendrup put in jail for deserting the summit party. Lives were at stake, not to mention the great and noble goal of placing a human being atop the second-highest mountain on Earth! Thanks to Cromwell, Durrance, and the Sherpas, Dudley Wolfe was alone at nearly 25,000 feet. Wolfe would sue them all when they got back to the United States, Wiessner threatened.

Cromwell protested weakly. It wasn't easy to make decisions when they had no idea what was happening at the top of the mountain. They had all agreed long ago that the porters would come on July 23. And if they wanted to talk about bad decisions, why did Wiessner leave Wolfe alone?

Wiessner couldn't find an answer that made sense. But at this point, it didn't matter. Wolfe was high on the mountain, and there was no reason to think he could get down by himself. Something had to be done.

But who had the strength to climb 8,000 feet and help a half-dead man to safety? Sheldon and Cranmer were long gone. Useless on the mountain, they had left a week earlier for Srinagar. Cromwell had never been above Camp IV. He was leaving with the porters the next day. Kikuli was still limping around on frostbitten feet. Pasang Lama had broken ribs and battered kidneys. Durrance was ravaged by the altitude whenever he climbed higher than Camp II.

As for Wiessner, he seemed to have lost touch with reality. He insisted that all he needed was a couple days' rest. Then he would climb to Camp VIII, pick up Wolfe, and make another attempt at the summit. "Maybe the Gods will be with me and let me have what is due to me," he wrote.

To everyone else at Base Camp, it was clear that the mountain gods had chewed up Fritz Wiessner and spit him out.

▲

The first attempt to rescue Dudley Wolfe began the next day, July 25. Durrance, Dawa, Pasang Kitar, and Phinsoo made it to Camp IV before Dawa collapsed with chest pains. Durrance limped back with Dawa in tow, leaving Kitar and Phinsoo with orders to keep climbing.

Back at Base Camp, Wiessner, Durrance, and Kikuli held a conference. It's not clear exactly how the decision was made, but on July 28 at 6:00 a.m., Pasang Kikuli shouldered a sleeping bag and some food and left Base Camp with Tsering Norbu. "Good luck for me to have a man like Pasang left," Wiessner would write later; "he is dependable and always does what he plans, I could not do it better."

On feet already ravaged by the cold, Kikuli led Tsering up 7,000 feet of snow, ice, and rock in a single day—through the loose scree above Camp II, up House's Chimney, and finally across the snow slopes to the tiny tent platforms of

Kikuli at Camp II, weeks before the rescue attempt.

Camp VI. There they found Kitar and Phinsoo already dug in. Kikuli and Tsering reconstructed a battered tent, fell inside, and slept.

The next day, Tsering stayed behind, sick from the rapid change in altitude the day before. Somehow, Kikuli was able to climb. He led Kitar and Phinsoo up the rock and ice of the Black Pyramid. Around noon, they stood outside Dudley Wolfe's tent at Camp VII.

At first, there was no sign of life. When Kikuli pushed the tent flap open, he was met by a terrible stench. Wolfe lay in his sleeping bag, listless and confused. He hadn't left the tent in days, even to go to the bathroom. His food lay strewn around the tent floor, ruined by his own waste. It had been several days since he'd been able to melt snow for drinking water. "I ran out of matches," he said in a hoarse whisper.

The Sherpas found a stove and brewed some tea for the Hermit of K2. Kikuli handed over a bundle of mail and a note from Wiessner, but Wolfe let them drop without reading a word.

It was time for Wolfe Sahib to go down, Kikuli said, and the Sherpas were there to help him. His friends were waiting for him at Base Camp.

With help from Kitar and Phinsoo, Kikuli nudged Wolfe out of the soiled tent and into the light. Wolfe squinted painfully. He staggered around the tent as best he could and then collapsed in the snow. He couldn't climb just this minute, he said. He needed a day to get his strength back. If they would come back tomorrow, he would be ready to descend.

At that moment, Kikuli must have known that Wolfe would never get off the mountain. As Durrance had discovered, climbers did not recover their strength at this altitude. They only got weaker. But what could he do? Sherpas simply did not order their employers around. He could try to persuade Wolfe Sahib, but he couldn't make him climb.

Before the sun fell too low in the sky, the Sherpas said goodbye to Dudley Wolfe. Without sleeping bags, they couldn't stay at Camp VII. They promised to return the next day and disappeared down the slope.

▲

More than 7,000 feet down the mountain, Durrance and Wiessner took turns peering through binoculars at the slope between Camps VI and VII. Before noon they had seen three tiny dots move up the slope. Around 5:30 p.m., they saw three climb down.

The mood at Base Camp darkened. The Sherpas had made it to VII after what must Have been an incredible feat of speed climbing. But where was Dudley Wolfe? Wiessner insisted it was nothing to worry about. Wolfe would be standing at Base Camp in two or three days, ready to begin the trek home.

Durrance didn't believe it, and he began to mope around the camp in a noticeably anxious state. Several porters who had stayed at Base Camp to help them clear out told Durrance he had been full of jokes on the march to the mountain. Now, they complained, he barely cracked a smile.

After a day of high winds and blinding snowfall, Wiessner and Durrance again peered up the slope, but clouds hid the high camps from view. The next day, too, they saw nothing.

Finally, at 7:30 on the morning of August 2, Durrance spotted a lone figure making its way down the rock and snow below Camp VI. By early afternoon, the figure appeared in Base Camp. It was Tsering Norbu, exhausted from a sprint down the mountain. When he managed to catch his breath, he told his story in broken English.

After waiting out the storm, Kikuli, Kitar, and Phinsoo had gone back to bring Wolfe Sahib down. Tsering waited for them all day and night. He waited the next day, calling up the mountain and hoping for a response. Finally, he gave up. He was in no condition to challenge the Black Pyramid by himself. And even if he made it to Camp VII, what would he find? Four men could not possibly survive two nights that high on the mountain with one sleeping bag and no food.

Fritz Wiessner, refusing to believe that he had lost four

men to K2, made one more desperate attempt to get up the mountain. But the rescue was doomed before it started. Tsering was exhausted and terrified of the mountain that had swallowed his three Sherpa companions. Dawa had shooting pains in his chest and could barely get a sound through his throat. No matter how deeply Wiessner breathed, it felt like oxygen never reached his lungs. The three men got as far as Camp II, where a storm pinned them down for four days. Finally, they staggered back to Base Camp.

▲

Depressed and defeated, the remains of the Second American Karakoram Expedition left on August 9 and started the long march out from under the shadow of K2.

By the time they left, Wolfe and his rescuers had been missing for 10 days with just one sleeping bag and no food. "It was certain," Wiessner would write in his first public account of the expedition, "that neither our brave Dudley Wolfe, whose determination and ability had grown the higher he went, nor the three unforgettable Sherpas, Pasang Kikuli, Pasang Kitar, and Phinsoo, who so gallantly had done their best to rescue their Sahib, could possibly be alive. They have, as their monument, a more beautiful structure than any man will ever erect, K2."

"A more beautiful structure than any man will ever erect."

PART THREE

1953
The Savage Mountain

The Third American Karakoram Expedition

Top, standing from left: Tony Streather, Charlie Houston, Bob Craig, George Bell, Bill White (NBC reporter), Pete Schoening, Bob Bates.

Seated from left: Dee Molenaar, Art Gilkey, Lieutenant Zaffir (military interpreter), Colonel Mohammad Ata-Ullah.

Bottom (names not in order): Hunza porters, Ghulam Mohammad, Kairal Hidayat, Haji Bey, Mohammad Ali, Hussain, and Vilyati.

11

No Superstars

To Charlie Houston's kids, Penny, Robin, and David, it felt like Christmas had never ended. In the spring of 1953, boxes arrived almost every day at their house in Exeter, New Hampshire. Each box had a new curiosity inside. There were ropes and metal clips called carabiners, boots with rubber cleats and crampons with 2-inch metal spikes, fluffy down jackets and wool socks that looked like they had been made for giants.

Then there was the food. Exotic food, magically transformed from its natural form into something else. For weeks the Houston kitchen had been a testing lab for a very strange feast. Boxes came packed with dehydrated meat bars—a pound of steak shrunk to four ounces of sinew. Potatoes and vegetables and soups had been dried and ground into powders. With a little water added, the powders congealed into something that a person might want to eat—if he happened to be stuck in a tent on the highest reaches of a mountain.

That, of course, is where Charlie Houston wanted to be. Ever since news of Wiessner's failure made it back to the states, Houston and Bob Bates had been dreaming about a return to K2. Now, it was finally going to happen.

It had been 14 years since Dudley Wolfe, Pasang Kikuli, Pasang Kitar, and Phinsoo vanished on K2. Since then, the world had come apart and pieced itself together again. Three weeks after Wiessner and Durrance trudged off the Baltoro Glacier and back to civilization, 1.5 million German soldiers stormed into Poland. World War II spread across the globe.

For at least six years, no one climbed mountains except soldiers looking for an advantage over enemy troops. During that time, at least 30 million people died on the battlefield and in German prison camps. Entire cities were leveled by firebombs. It was enough to make most of the world forget the deaths of one wealthy American adventurer and three professional mountain porters from Nepal.

But Charlie Houston remembered.

▲

One evening in 1940, while war raged across the ocean, Houston heard the whole story from Jack Durrance. Durrance had been back for several months, and the nightmare on K2 haunted him. He came to Exeter and spent hours slumped in a chair, recounting the ordeal. He talked without emotion. He looked like a beaten man.

After they left Base Camp, Durrance and Wiessner had spent nearly three weeks trekking back to Srinagar. Wiessner was completely spent. Some days, he stopped in the middle of the trail, collapsed on a rock in the sun, and napped. All the while, Durrance and Wiessner kept their distance. They spoke just enough to put together a report

Wiessner in 1939, resting on the trek out from the mountain.

to the American Alpine Club, explaining the disaster on the mountain.

When they got to Srinagar, Cromwell was waiting for them. He read the report and lashed out in anger at Wiessner. The report blamed no one, but Cromwell thought he knew beyond a doubt who was responsible. Wiessner had let Dudley Wolfe climb far higher than he should have and then left him behind when he couldn't get down. Cromwell told Wiessner to his face that he should be charged with murder. Then he fired off a letter to the AAC telling his side of the story.

Durrance realized they could be heading for a vicious public battle over what had happened on the mountain. He sent a telegram to George Sheldon, telling him not to talk to anyone about the expedition. He said goodbye to Wiessner, who boarded a plane to Egypt before coming home. "Fritz and I part ways," Durrance wrote in his diary. Then he added, "thank god."

By the time everyone got back home, rumors were flying. People in the climbing community wanted to know what had gone wrong. Dudley Wolfe's brother hired a lawyer, who grilled Wiessner, Durrance, Cranmer, Sheldon, and Cromwell. The AAC formed a committee to investigate what had happened on the mountain.

Everyone had an opinion about Wiessner. The British mountaineering expert Kenneth Mason blamed him for valuing the summit over the safety of his climbing partners. It was "criminal" that Wiessner didn't turn around earlier and take everyone home, Mason said.

Others, like the American climber Robert Underhill, idolized Wiessner for his skill and determination. "Wiessner, with Wolfe behind him, was the only one who still wanted to climb the mountain," Underhill wrote. "He had the guts! And there is no single thing finer in a climber, or in a man."

A climber. Or a man. The Wiessner expedition had opened a debate that wasn't just about climbing. It was about life. Who are these people who risk their lives to get to the top of a mountain? Are they heroes or reckless fools? When human beings are stretched to their absolute limits, are they responsible for their companions or only for themselves? On a mountaineering expedition—and in life—is it the goal that matters or the way you get there?

Rumor had it that before leaving Base Camp, Wiessner had announced where he stood on these questions. He was run-down and frustrated that he couldn't climb. His partners were demanding to know why he left Wolfe on the mountainside to die. According to George Trench, Wiessner blurted out, "A Himalayan mountain is like war! You must expect a few casualties."

In the end, no one was charged with murder. The AAC's

report failed to assign blame for the deaths. Instead, it said that "weak administration" caused a breakdown in communication on the mountain.

To Wiessner, that seemed unfair. He protested and blamed the disaster on Durrance for stripping the camps. Then he resigned from the AAC, went back to his ski wax business, and paid off most of his debt to Wolfe's family.

Publicly, Charlie Houston steered clear of all the Wiessner talk. But he knew what he thought about the expedition. In his view, Wiessner had refused to accept that his team didn't have the skill to climb K2. He drove them beyond their ability to cope with the mountain. And by leaving Dudley Wolfe alone high on the slopes of K2, he had broken the sacred bond between climbers—the fellowship of the rope.

"Wiessner is to blame for most if not all of the mishap, and I don't believe I can ever forgive him," Charlie wrote to a friend. "I didn't know Wolfe, but I knew and dearly loved Pasang and Phinsoo, and what they so gallantly did, *alone*, I can't forget."

▲

Late in 1952, as Charlie Houston planned his return to K2, Kikuli and the others were still on his mind. So before the boxes started arriving, a parade of mountaineers in their 20s and 30s showed up at Houston's doorstep. There were

25 men in all, narrowed down from a list of 40. Each one wanted a chance to climb K2, and Houston was going to pick them carefully. He was determined not to repeat Wiessner's mistakes.

As Charlie and Bob Bates interviewed the men one by one, they knew what they wanted. Sure, everyone had to have climbing skills. But more importantly, they had to be good companions. There would be no superstars on this trip—only men who could work as a team. Houston knew that altitude brought out the worst in people. He needed tentmates who wouldn't hate each other after they'd been trapped in a storm for three days straight.

By the beginning of 1953, five men had made the cut. Rumor had it that Houston's golden retriever, Honey, made the final decisions. The climbers she liked were going to K2.

▲

In the middle of May 1953, Pete Schoening stepped off a bus into the crowds at New York City's Penn Station. Known as an expert rock climber, he'd been on a couple of long expeditions in Alaska and had passed the golden retriever test in Exeter. But he had never attempted anything like K2. At 25, he was the baby of the expedition, and he wasn't sure how well he fit in. He had grown up in Seattle, and New York felt too big and busy. The luminaries at the AAC had a party planned for the climbers, and Schoening wasn't looking forward to it. "There is plenty of

Schoening (left) and Molenaar (second from right) with two members of the 1953 Everest expedition, George Lowe and Edmund Hillary.

swanking in this part of the country," he wrote to his parents. "Too stuffed shirt for me."

Schoening met the rest of the team in New York as they arrived from all across the country. There was George Bell, a research physicist who worked on top secret projects at Los Alamos, New Mexico, where the first atomic bomb was made. At six foot five, he towered over Pete. But like Schoening, he didn't say much in a crowd.

Bob Craig, on the other hand, loved to make people laugh. He was teaching skiing to soldiers and working on his PhD in philosophy when he got the invite from Houston.

INTO THE CLOUDS

His friend Dee Molenaar arrived in New York from the West Coast. Molenaar had climbed with Craig out west and worked with him training troops. A geologist and a painter, he had his sketch pad and watercolors packed with his crampons and climbing boots.

Together the climbers suffered through a couple of days of "swanky" dinners, interviews with journalists, and last-minute shopping for gear. The night before they left New York, Schoening and Molenaar slept at the tiny Manhattan apartment of their last team member. Art Gilkey was about a year older than Schoening. He was a dedicated geology student who spent his summers doing research in the mountains. He seemed to do everything with a quiet intensity. That night, Gilkey stayed up late working on his PhD thesis while Schoening and Molenaar crashed in the next room.

The next day, the team gathered at the airport. They were happy to be done with their time in New York. But when they finally got ready to board the plane, their suitcases were too heavy for airline regulations. They had to pull out 240 pounds of gear and stuff it in their pockets and carry-on bags.

As the plane lifted off, no one was more excited than Charlie Houston. It had been a long time coming, but he was finally going back to K2. Houston had spent World

War II working with fighter pilots, and sometimes at the military base, he would imagine himself in the Himalaya. "When the low clouds are grey and stormy," he wrote to Bates in 1942, "and the rising or setting sun picks out a snowy white thunder head high above and makes it look like a great Himalaya from Darjeeling or Kashmir, well, when that happens I just about burst into tears."

Houston still believed that the challenge of climbing was more important than the goal. He loved the mountains for their beauty, for the physical test they posed, for the friendships made there. But he also desperately wanted to get to the top.

The war had been over for eight years, and the race for the 8,000-meter peaks was on again. In 1950, the first of the giant mountains had fallen. Two French climbers lost fingers and toes doing it, but they made it to the 26,545-foot summit of Annapurna. As Houston and his team crossed the ocean, a British expedition was making its way up Everest.

K2 was the best hope for the United States. In January, the *Boston Globe* had run a story about the expedition. FOR THE AMERICANS, K-2 MUST DO, read the headline. Houston, who took everything he did seriously, felt the pressure. "We will try to let nothing short of a world war stop us," he wrote to the head of the AAC.

INTO THE CLOUDS

A few seats away, Dee Molenaar knew it would take a lot less than that to stop him. He already missed his wife, Lee, and his little daughter, Patti. Lee was proud that he'd been chosen for the team, but she was reluctant to see him go. "Be careful," she had said to him when he left Seattle for New York. "Don't take any chances."

12

Back to the Mountain

Bob Bates thought they were going to die before they made it to K2. He was 15,000 feet in the air, staring out the window of a cargo plane. At that altitude, you might expect to fly clear of any obstacles on Earth.

Not in the Himalaya.

In 1938, Bates and Houston had covered this part of the expedition on foot. Now, they were flying the 180 miles from Rawalpindi to Skardu, and the last half of the ride took them through a landscape unlike any other. The plane wove through a towering skyline of mountain spires. It skimmed 15,000-foot ridges. It dove through gorges that narrowed enough to sheer the wings off if a gust of wind came up unannounced.

Bates and Houston remembered this mystical wonderland from 1938, and they were ecstatic to be back. But even from a plane, you could feel the danger in the landscape below. Fifty miles outside of Skardu, they veered around the snow-covered bulk of Nanga Parbat. Journalists now called it the "Killer Mountain" because of its tragic history.

The climbers pressed their noses against the windows and tried to pick out landmarks. There was the Rakhiot Ridge, where Mummery became the first mountaineer to vanish in the Himalaya and nine more climbers were lost in 1934. And there, maybe, was the site of Camp IV, where a midnight avalanche smothered 16 climbers in their tents in 1937. More than 30 lives had been lost on Nanga Parbat, and no one had reached its 26,660-foot summit.

K2 stood another 1,600 feet higher.

The "Killer Mountain": Nanga Parbat from the window of the cargo plane.

With Nanga Parbat behind them, the plane cleared a final ridge and plummeted like a stone. Just when it seemed they were going to nose-dive into the Earth, they leveled off. The plane skimmed a pasture so close it nearly took out a few cows. Then it rumbled to a stop on a strip of dirt known as the Skardu airport.

▲

On the way into Skardu, the climbers felt like returning heroes, even though they hadn't set foot on K2 yet. The entire village of 7,000 turned out to welcome them. Schoolchildren lined the road into town. They cheered and draped necklaces of flowers around the Americans. Pakistan was one of the world's newest nations. India had won its independence from Britain in 1947, and two years later, Pakistan had been carved out of its borders to give India's Muslim population a homeland. The people of Skardu wanted the Americans to support their young nation when they returned home. A loud chant went up from the crowd: "Pakistan *zinzabad*! America *zinzabad*!" ("Long live Pakistan! Long live America!")

Houston and the others enjoyed the welcome. But as they got ready to leave for the mountain, they had a sinking feeling that beyond the borders of this tiny town, no one cared about their expedition anymore. The rest of the world was too busy celebrating the conquest of a different mountain. Everest had been summited.

INTO THE CLOUDS

The news had made it to Rawalpindi before they boarded their plane: On May 29, the Sherpa climber Tenzing Norgay and a beekeeper from New Zealand named Edmund Hillary fought their way to the highest point on Earth. Ten expeditions had failed on Everest. Fifteen climbers had died trying. Now, two men had spent 15 minutes at 29,028 feet, looking down on the world.

Houston and the others knew the rest of the world was riveted. The London *Times* devoted a special 32-page section to the climb. The queen of England received the news

Reading the news in Rawalpindi.

through diplomatic channels. Hillary was knighted before he even got off the mountain.

What was left to do? True climbers knew that K2 was a more difficult mountain than Everest. But most of the world didn't care. What mattered were the superlatives— and in mountain climbing, tallest was the one that counted. Even if Houston and the others managed to survive the cold and the wind; even if they conquered the rock, ice, and snow; even if they fought their way to the top—they would still be standing 780 feet below the throne carved out by Hillary and Norgay. As the *Boston Globe* put it five months earlier, "A conquest of K2 by Americans is not going to bring any avalanche of fame if the British make the grade with Everest, the monarch of them all."

But fame wasn't what had brought Charlie Houston back to K2. He was there to test himself against one of the most demanding challenges nature had to offer. He allowed himself a moment of regret. Then he sent his congratulations to the British team by telegram.

Dee Molenaar found a reason to be happy about the news. "Now K2 is highest unclimbed mtn. on earth," he wrote in his diary. "We're determined to carry on our plans as before."

▲

On June 5, the Third American Karakoram Expedition dropped all news of the outside world and began the march to K2. The world they were leaving behind had completely transformed since 1938. But as they made their way out of the village, it seemed as though nothing had changed in centuries. There were no roads—only narrow mountain trails and dusty plains. They crossed one river on a raft made from inflated goatskins. At three more, they held their breath and wobbled across on the infamous 300-foot rope bridges. With every step, it seemed, they traveled back in time.

The porters who followed them into the mountains only added to the feeling. There were 90 of them, bent under the weight of 60-pound loads. They carried an odd assortment of crates and bundles, all of it bound together and strapped to their backs with goat-hair rope.

They seemed to come from a different century than the Western sahibs. Houston and his team marched ahead wearing waterproof boots, windproof parkas, and Eddie Bauer jackets filled with soft, warm goose down. The porters had leather mukluks between their feet and the harsh landscape of rocks and river crossings. Many of them simply went barefoot. They carried thin shawls to huddle under when the mountain air got cold. This time at least, Houston had a supply of snow goggles to hand out when they reached the blinding glare of the glacier ice.

It was an odd, unbalanced relationship between the porters and these men of privilege who came to their homeland with money to spend and backbreaking work to hire out.

The porters had no camp stoves to cook on. For the last week of the trek, where there were no trees, they carried firewood on their backs.

The two groups waged a tense battle for power on the trail. Every couple of days the porters refused to move an inch until they were promised more money. A few days into the trek, gear started to disappear—a pair of boots here, an ice axe there. The Americans kept one-hour watches through the night. By the end of the trek, the porters were begging for clothes, food, and shoes.

It didn't help that the two groups spoke different languages. Negotiations took place with a lot of arm waving and one-word sentences. A British transport officer named Tony Streather had joined the team, and it was his job to organize the porters. But everyone had to communicate daily with the men who carried their gear. Molenaar came with a list of Hindustani phrases in his diary: *saf pani lao* for "bring clean water"; *jaldi karo* for "do it quickly." Also included was an essential term for campfire conversation: *padd,* the word for "fart."

▲

In the late afternoon of June 19, after a final 12-mile slog up the Godwin-Austen Glacier, the porters set down their loads for good. Underfoot was a jumble of jagged black rock. Overhead rose the snow-dusted ridges of K2. The expedition had arrived at Base Camp.

The climbers had gotten their first glimpse of the mountain that morning at a spot called Concordia, where two giant glaciers combine into one. In front of them to the north, giant walls of rock and ice rose from the ground and disappeared behind a bank of clouds. Higher up— impossibly high, it seemed—the summit floated above the clouds. A mile-long trail of snow and ice crystals blew from the peak like a giant banner.

Nearly every climber who has stood on this spot has felt paralyzed by the sight. "Nothing on the whole planet matches it," one wrote.

Bob Craig stared at the great plume of snow trailing from the peak and wondered what the wind up there would do to a man. He thought the mountain looked impossible to climb. Dee Molenaar was struggling for breath at this point, trying his best to keep putting one foot in front of the other. "Looks very steep and rugged" was all he could manage when he sat down with his diary that night.

That evening, the temperature plummeted and snow began to fall. Pete Schoening's fingers went numb as he tried to write to his parents. The climbers worried about the porters with their bare feet and thin clothes. Tony Streather offered up tea, warm food, and a two-person tent for a couple of especially weak-looking men. Six porters piled into the tent. The rest built low walls of stone to block the wind. They huddled under blankets and tarps, and somehow survived the night.

The next day, Streather paid the porters and they trudged down the glacier toward home. He was relieved to see them go after two weeks of constant negotiation. As the last porter faded from view, Base Camp grew quiet. Fifteen men were left standing in a sea of crates—eight climbers, six high-altitude porters, and a Pakistani official named Mohammad Ata-Ullah, who would be in charge of Base Camp during their time on the mountain.

The men had food for 70 days. The porters would return in 50. Until then, K2 was their home, and their nearest neighbor was 100 miles away.

The view from Base Camp, at the foot of K2.

13

Ghosts of K2

On the morning of June 21, Charlie Houston watched eight men set off up the glacier with 25- to 40-pound loads on their backs. The supply train was under way. One camp at a time, they would move up the mountain, leaving each tiny haven stocked with food, stoves, sleeping bags, and tents. The plan was to get 250 pounds of supplies to 25,000 feet—enough to get eight men through two weeks. Then they would stock one more camp with a single tent and supplies for a summit team of two.

They would not, Houston had vowed many times over, repeat Wiessner's mistakes. His team would climb together or not at all. No advance party would get too far ahead of the supplies.

They made steady progress in the first couple of weeks. The work was hard but the weather held. Some days the sun turned the snow to slush. They took turns breaking trail and sunk to their knees with every step. Other days

Molenaar's painting of the mountain from the south, with the team's planned route up the Abruzzi Ridge.

the wind blew cold and fierce, forcing them to kick steps in the crust with their crampons.

To Houston, the steady march up the mountain was both thrilling and frightening. It felt so final every time they packed their sleeping bags and stoves and broke trail for a new camp. His wife, Dorcas, and the kids and everything familiar faded further into the distance. One camp after another, they traded the known for the unknown.

Along the way, each of the men responded differently to the altitude. Molenaar was the hardest hit. His muscles ached, his head throbbed, and he had no desire to eat. Gilkey and Houston had headaches. Craig was a little moody. Streather felt fine now that the porters were gone. Bates was his usual cheerful self, and Schoening looked strong and eager to work. Bell was unflappable; he acted like he'd just been out for a hike in the park.

No one knew exactly how he was going to react as he climbed. But since the 1939 expedition, a lot had been learned about what happens to the body at altitude. Houston himself had spent the war studying how fighter pilots reacted to high-altitude flights. He knew that the body adjusts as it climbs. Red blood cells increase to make up for the lack of oxygen in each breath.

The Everest expedition had help from bottled oxygen on the highest slopes. Hillary and Norgay had strapped tanks to their backs and breathed air that felt as rich as it did at sea level. Houston had decided against the artificial help. Hauling oxygen tanks to K2 would have required a much bigger expedition. And oxygen-aided climbers didn't acclimatize as well as they would on their own. If the tanks failed on a final summit push, the consequences could be fatal.

As Houston's team climbed into the highest reaches of K2, they would breathe the air the mountain had to offer. They would acclimatize in stages—a couple of days of misery, followed by relief, then misery again. At some point—25,000 feet for some, lower for others—there would be nothing but a slow decline. As Jack Durrance had discovered in 1939, in the Himalaya you never fully recover.

▲

On June 28, with Camp I fully stocked, Houston, Craig, and Bell clambered up a steep slope of loose rock, searching for the old Camp II. After a couple hours' climb, they came across a nearly level piece of ground that looked as though a garbage can had been overturned on it. A few cans of jam and pemmican lay scattered in the snow, hardly rusted at all. Nearby was a stove, a 5-pound can of Ovaltine, and a rumpled Logan tent.

At their feet were the first reminders of Wiessner's doomed expedition—not that Charlie Houston needed reminding. He knew they would be climbing in the footsteps of Dudley Wolfe and Pasang Kikuli.

It was an eerie thought. No one had set foot on K2 since

Durrance and Wiessner gave up on their lost friends and limped off the mountain. And the Himalaya preserves its history in gruesome ways. George Mallory, who nearly made it to the top of Everest in 1924, was found 75 years later at 27,000 feet, a name tag still readable on his flannel shirt.

At the newly found Camp II, Houston, Craig, and Bell couldn't resist pitching the Logan tent and piling in. Was it here, inside the same canvas walls, that Wiessner had shivered through the night with Pasang Lama after leaving Wolfe at Camp VII? And if the mountain had preserved a tent untouched for 14 years, what else might lay hidden on its slopes? Houston knew that in the days to come, he could cross the base of a gully or crest a plateau and find the body of his friend Pasang Kikuli, frozen stiff in the snow.

▲

Dee Molenaar and the rest of the team spent June 30 hauling loads to Camp II. When Molenaar returned to Camp I, he was spent. He'd been out for eight hours. His legs barely held up his body. As he relaxed at camp, he heard a low growl high on the mountain. The growl built to a thundering roar, which finally materialized into a churning mass of snow, ice, and rock. Well within view, the mass hurtled down a gully and across the glacier until it slammed into the mountain wall on the other side and erupted in a billowing white cloud that climbed a third of a mile up the mountain.

INTO THE CLOUDS

They were all starting to expect anything from K2. But it still rattled the nerves. The mountain, ancient as it was, felt alive at times. The glacier cracked and popped as the ice shifted underfoot. Snow piled on the slopes until gravity tugged it into giant avalanches. Lead climbers unleashed a barrage of loose rock on their unlucky teammates below.

It wasn't long before another avalanche rumbled down the mountain even closer to Molenaar's tent and dusted the camp with snow. "Too close," he wrote in his diary that night.

An avalanche tumbles off Broad Peak onto the glacier across from Camp I.

Since Base Camp, Molenaar had been fighting a private battle with his nerves. Schoening and Craig, Bell and Gilkey—they seemed to be climbing with ease. But for Molenaar, most days were a struggle. The headaches came and went. He never slept well. By the end of the day, his knees felt weak and his lungs craved oxygen. The loads, it seemed, only got heavier as the team worked its way toward House's Chimney, the gateway to K2's upper slopes.

Molenaar and the others were, in fact, carrying heavier loads than they had expected. Before the trip, Houston had been hoping for a team of Sherpa porters, expert climbers like Kikuli and Phinsoo. But Pakistan had given him a team from the region of Hunza. There were six men— Ghulam Mohammad, Kairal Hidayat, Haji Bey, Mohammad Ali, Hussain, and Vilyati. Only one had experience at high altitudes, and Houston wasn't planning to take the group past Camp IV.

That meant extra work the Americans hadn't planned for. Even at the lower camps, they gave the Hunzas lighter loads to keep them from quitting. Still, headaches, back-aches, or snow blindness put the porters out of action for a day here, a day there. Schoening, who was always willing to shoulder the heaviest load, thought some of the Hunzas were "playing sick."

Molenaar worried he wasn't pulling his share of the load either. He had his good days, but he needed more rest time than Schoening or Gilkey, who never seemed to get tired. Each day, he spent more and more time thinking of his family. Pretty soon, he was carrying a secret with him into the tents at night. He didn't admit it to the others, but he was ready to get off the mountain. Two days after the avalanche, he confided to his diary: "Thinking of long climb ahead, many load relays, often wish mid-August was here & we were heading home. I miss Lee & Patti terribly. No more expeditions for me!"

▲

A week later, on July 9, Charlie Houston followed Molenaar up a craggy cliffside at 21,000 feet. The days had been long and the nights restless for everyone, and Houston knew Molenaar was struggling. But today, Dee seemed eager to lead. He moved up and to the left, pounding pitons into the rock face where he could and clipping his rope into the holes for protection. Behind him, Houston and George Bell followed, their arms and legs spread wide, clutching at tiny holds with their fingers and toes.

Finally, they pulled themselves onto the top of the ridge and paused to catch their breath. For the moment, Molenaar hardly looked like a man who wanted to go home. From now on, they agreed, the pitch would be known as "Molenaar's Madness."

After a final scramble up a tall rock pinnacle, the three men stood staring up at an 80-foot cliff with a single,

Fixed ropes on a dangerous traverse above Camp II.

snow-filled chute carved into its face. After 20 days haul-ing supplies up the lower half of the mountain, they had made it to House's Chimney.

Houston had been thinking about this moment for days. Like Molenaar, he'd been secretly wondering whether he was out of his depth on K2. He knew he was a good leader, but he wasn't sure he could navigate the rock and ice like the others. In 1938, he'd given up a couple thousand feet below the summit. Now, most of his teammates were both younger and more skilled. Maybe he didn't belong out here anymore.

House's Chimney was K2's most difficult obstacle, and Houston had decided it would be his test. As they looked up the rock face, they could see pitons and fixed ropes from '38 and '39 wedged into the crack. But they were use-less now, unreliable and frozen into the cliffside. Someone would have to lead the climb, fixing new ropes to pro-tect climbers on the way up. Molenaar or Bell—both better climbers than Houston—were the obvious choices, but Houston had another plan.

He tried to sound casual about it. "Would you fellows mind too much if I tried to lead this?" he asked.

With Bell and Molenaar belaying him from below, Houston started up the chimney. He chose his holds care-fully, trying not to look as clumsy as he felt. When he paused to gasp for air, he pretended to adjust the rope or

Molenaar and Craig at the base of House's Chimney.

blow his nose. The crack widened, and he spread his limbs and levered himself up. Near the top, it narrowed again. His forearms throbbed and his lungs heaved, but he hauled himself over the lip and onto the crest of the ridge.

He was dizzy with exhaustion, but as Charlie Houston sat on the ridge and caught his breath, a wave of satisfaction rose inside him. In a moment, he would help Bell and Molenaar up. They would drop their loads and climb back down to rejoin the others. But right now, laid out below was one of the most sublime views on Earth. Two glaciers, ancient boulevards of snow and ice, met a mile below, winding through a vast field of snowy spires. Masherbrum's 25,600-foot peak towered over them all. The mountain under Houston's feet rose more than 2,500 feet higher, and he had just conquered one of the hardest routes it had to offer. Now, if only the weather would cooperate, he knew he could handle the rest.

"Come on up," he yelled down. "I've got you belayed like a house."

▲

They said goodbye to the Hunzas on July 13. There were hugs all around, managed around thick down parkas and stiff nylon shells. The Hunzas left for Base Camp, where they would spend the rest of the expedition with the Pakistani colonel Ata-Ullah.

The Americans turned to finish ferrying supplies to

Camp IV so they could get the entire group up House's Chimney and leave the bottom half of the mountain behind. From here on, they would get weather reports from Ata-Ullah over the radio. Otherwise, they were on their own. On Everest, Edmund Hillary had a huge team of Sherpas and British climbers lugging supplies most of the way up the mountain. On K2, Houston now had only his seven teammates.

That night, the first big storm of the season rolled in and pounded the mountainside. For two days the team lay trapped in their tents at Camps II, III, and IV. Molenaar huddled with George Bell at IV. The wind blew so hard they couldn't leave the tent. They had to pee in a peanut can and dump it out the door. To pass the time, they swapped stories about their childhoods. Molenaar read and pored over pictures of Lee and Patti. But no matter what they did, the confinement drove him crazy.

Below, at Camp III, Houston dreamed he was trapped between two blocks of ice, smothering to death. He woke to find the tent wall pressed against his face under a pile of snow. Outside, blowing snow had collected between the tent and the mountain wall. Houston rolled to the center and woke his tentmate, Tony Streather. Someone had to brave the wind to shovel or the tent would be pushed off its narrow platform and slide down the mountain with its residents inside.

Houston drew straws with Streather and lost. He

Digging out the tent at Camp III during the storm.

bundled himself into frozen boots and a parka, grumbling all the way. Hugging the sides of the tent so he wouldn't be blown off the platform, he managed to shovel the tent clear. He climbed back in, making sure to dust Streather's face with snow so his tentmate knew exactly what the weather was like out there.

▲

By July 16, the men were moving again, and the gloom lifted for Molenaar. "Sunshine, warmth make attitude entirely different," he wrote. "K2 seems friendly now. On to Camp V!"

But for everyone on the mountain, the mood had shifted. Fifteen people had been living on K2 for nearly a month. They still had food and fuel, but the supplies shrank with every passing day. And the weather had a way of ruining the best-laid plans. They had been trapped in their tents for two days, and there had been worse storms in the Himalaya. This one had simply given them a small taste of what the mountain could do to an expedition.

On July 21, they got another reminder. The entire team packed loads up a steep snow slope that ended in a tall rock

Bates with the bundles left at Camp VI by Kikuli, Kitar, and Phinsoo before their last attempt to bring Dudley Wolfe down.

buttress. At the base of the wall, Bates and Houston stood staring at a sight they would never forget. On the ground lay the remains of three tents. Next to the shredded canvas were three sleeping bags, laid out in a row, each of them strapped on a pack frame with other supplies—a stove, a bundle of tea wrapped in a bandana and packed in a box. They were standing in the middle of Wiessner's Camp VI.

Fourteen years ago, on a cold, misty morning, Pasang Kikuli, Pasang Kitar, and Phinsoo had put the bundles together before they left to get Dudley Wolfe. They would be back soon, they told Tsering Norbu. And if they had Wolfe Sahib with them, they would need to get him down the mountain quickly.

Then they climbed into the mist.

Fourteen years later, the bundles were still there, waiting.

14

Three Good Days

harlie Houston shivered on a small ledge at the top of the Black Pyramid, somewhere below Dudley Wolfe's final camp. Just a few feet away, the snow-crusted rocks dropped off into a steep ice slope that plummeted 7,000 feet before leveling off. It was bitterly cold. The wind cut through Houston's parka. He could feel his feet begin to numb inside his boots.

It was July 27, and Houston, George Bell, and Bob Craig were making the team's first real push above Camp VI. The climbing had been hard, and Houston was exhausted. For 1,000 vertical feet, the three men had pulled themselves up on tiny, ice-covered holds in the rock. They had gone hours without a ledge big enough to rest on. Even if they had found one, the wind would have forced them to move in seconds.

It was grueling work, but it was climbing at its best.

Houston had felt the world drop away until there was only the rock in front of him. Identify a move and execute it. Identify the next move. Execute it. For minutes, even hours, life was detail: Left hand up, right foot over; rope slack, rope taut; the clink of hammer on piton.

It was a kind of freedom, this pure concentration. In danger you find peace. Maybe this was why they climbed.

While Houston rested on his ledge, Bell and Craig probed above him to the edge of the ice field that rose from the top of the Pyramid. They tried to find a trace of Wiessner's Camp VII or another spot level enough to pitch their own tents. Now it was late, they were tired, and they needed to get down.

As they climbed down to rejoin Houston, Bell chose a foothold on a boulder that looked solid. But when he transferred his weight, the boulder rolled. Bell landed with a thud on the ice and started to slide. Craig yelled a quick warning to Houston and watched with alarm as Bell clawed and scraped at the slope with his axe. Craig was in no position to belay Bell. If the rope between them went taut, they would both tumble into free fall down the jagged slope of the Black Pyramid.

Finally, Bell's axe dug deep enough and brought him to a stop, facedown in the ice. Bell and Craig collected themselves and climbed down to Houston, who had hugged the side of the slope while the boulder careened past, picking

On the Black Pyramid, high above the Godwin-Austen Glacier.

up speed as it battered its way down the cliff. Craig was obviously shaken as he told Houston what had happened.

"Pretty slippery spot" was all they could get out of Bell.

As they turned to descend the icy rock face, all trace of the quiet satisfaction Houston had felt on the morning climb was gone. His feet and hands were numb from cold. It still took all the concentration he could muster to find holds he could trust and cling to them. But the descent felt like it would never end.

By the time they limped into Camp VI that night, Houston was cold, exhausted, and flirting with frostbite. He collapsed into his sleeping bag and let Bates try to massage his hands and feet back to life.

▲

The next day a storm descended on Camp VI. Trapped in his tent with a bitter wind howling outside, Dee Molenaar spent the day asking himself a question: What would he sacrifice to get to the top of K2? Like most of his tentmates, he wasn't eating much. Altitude steals the appetite from climbers just when they need the calories most. Molenaar figured he was down to 155 pounds. He could see his own ribs.

Every day, it seemed, the weather got worse. Storms had kept them pinned down four days out of the last seven. Today, Molenaar tried to paint, but he couldn't keep at it.

Whenever he sat up, the wind-battered tent beat against his head.

Despite the weather, the mood in camp was good. Streather told stories about his adventures during the war. Bates was his usual optimistic self. Even today, after nearly losing his feet to frostbite, Houston was full of energy.

But everyone knew that the stakes were getting higher by the day. They were down to 18 days' worth of food, and they still hadn't found a place for Camp VII. At some point, time would force them to climb in weather like this, and what would happen then? The sun had been out yesterday, and Houston still came back with his feet frozen.

Molenaar could tell that everyone was asking themselves the same question he was: What, exactly, would they risk? Just three years ago, the French climber Maurice Herzog had answered that question in dramatic fashion near the top of Annapurna. Every climber knew the story well, and right now, with the wind howling outside the tents and Houston's feet still thawing out, it seemed especially relevant to Molenaar.

Herzog had stood a few hundred feet below the summit of Annapurna when his climbing partner, Louis Lachenal, wanted to turn back. Herzog refused. He was nearly delirious from the altitude, and the summit seemed to him like a sacred quest—an 8,000-meter peak, finally within reach. "In an hour or two, perhaps, victory would be ours," he wrote later. "Must we give up? Impossible! My whole being revolted against the idea . . . Today, we were consecrating an ideal, and no sacrifice was too great."

Herzog and Lachenal made it—the first climbers ever to stand atop an 8,000-meter peak. Then the descent turned into a nightmare. Herzog lost his gloves and he was too far gone to realize he could have replaced them with a spare pair of wool socks. Two days later he and Lachenal stumbled into Base Camp. They had survived an avalanche and a night in a crevasse without a tent. By that time, Herzog's hands and feet were blocks of ice. He had to be carried off the mountain by a relay of Sherpas.

Millions of people knew the story's conclusion. By 1953, Herzog's book about Annapurna had become a bestseller. Just before Molenaar left in May, the author had been touring the United States, telling his story. He limped from event to event, clutching his notes with hands that were little more than stumps. All his fingers and toes had been amputated.

That was not the end Molenaar had in mind for himself. He made a vow to his diary: Even after months of planning and weeks of effort on the mountain, he would know when to turn around. He could only hope his climbing partners would do the same. If anyone pushed himself beyond his limits, it would place a huge burden on the rest of the team. "Bringing an injured man down K2," he wrote, "would be an <u>extremely</u> difficult, if not impossible, task."

▲

By the afternoon of July 30, Houston was feeling desperate. It had been nearly 10 days since they established Camp VI. Getting eight men up the mountain had begun to seem like an impossible task. He stood with the rest of the team at the base of the ice slope above the Black Pyramid, huddled in his parka against the wind. Schoening and Gilkey had spent the day searching the slope for a Camp VII site. All they needed was a piece of ground big enough for three

Herzog's fingers were amputated on the long trek across Nepal after his ordeal.

tents and level enough to keep them all from sliding down the mountain in the middle of the night.

K2 had given them nothing.

Schoening and Gilkey didn't care. They had gotten this far; they weren't going back. They found a soft spot in the snow and hacked at it with their ice axes until they had the narrowest of platforms carved into the slope. It was 6 feet long and 3 feet wide, barely big enough for two men to sleep side by side. But for the two youngest members of the team, that was enough. They would spend the night there and resume the search for Camp VII in the morning.

Houston didn't like it. Neither did Molenaar. It was bitter cold, and the tiny platform offered no protection from the wind. A 600-foot incline, dangerously steep, loomed above the camp. If fresh snow fell during the night, there was no guarantee the slope would hold it. This was the avalanche slope that had terrified Tse Tendrup in 1939, and the slope where his friends were probably swept to their deaths.

But Houston knew they were running out of choices. And Schoening and Gilkey were a force. All the way up the mountain, Schoening had been the first one out the tent door, even in the worst weather. Gilkey was almost as young and even more eager. According to Molenaar, he wanted the summit "at all costs."

Houston reluctantly agreed that the two men should stay, just for a night. He and the rest of the team left a radio set in the tiny tent, dumped their loads just below the camp, and headed down the mountain.

Schoening and Gilkey crammed themselves into the tent. "Charlie is like a mother and is worried about me and Art," Schoening scribbled in his diary. Then he tried to sleep.

▲

The next day dawned cold and windy at Camp VI. New snow blanketed the mountain, and everyone woke worried about Schoening and Gilkey. Streather and Molenaar made a trip to Camp V to bring up two more loads of food. In the afternoon they piled into the large Army expedition tent and told stories to pass the time. Late in the afternoon, the radio crackled to life, and everyone gathered around.

Schoening and Gilkey announced from their cramped tent that they were cold, but alive and well. They had spent the day combing the ice slope, bundled into every piece of clothing they had. The climbing was slow and treacherous. For an hour at a time, Gilkey had shivered in place, belaying while Schoening kicked or chopped steps in the slope. Then Gilkey would follow and take the lead for an hour. At almost 25,000 feet, cutting steps was grueling work, but at least it kept the blood flowing. Standing in one place paying out rope, you felt like you could freeze into the slope—a serac made from human flesh.

All morning they had traversed the slope, searching for the camp where Wolfe had spent his last days. Finally, they decided it had been swept away by an avalanche. They retraced their steps to the tiny ledge and headed straight up the mountain. For 150 feet they chopped steps in the ice. The crusty ice turned to snow, and they made

At Camp VI, clinging to the side of the mountain below the Black Pyramid.

their way cautiously for another 400 feet. With each step, they sunk to their knees, half expecting the mass of powder to give way and pull them tumbling down the mountainside.

By midafternoon the ground leveled off, and they emerged onto a broad, gently sloping shoulder. Not since the lowest camps had the mountain given them this kind of space. To Schoening it felt like a breakthrough. They had taken the worst K2 had to offer and passed the test. Schoening and Gilkey picked a campsite that was out of avalanche danger. They dumped 20-pound loads and climbed down to their tent, where they had left the radio set.

They hadn't found Wiessner's Camp VII, Schoening told Houston. But they had discovered something better: a site for Camp VIII. From there, Schoening couldn't quite see the summit, but he was convinced they would get there.

All they needed were three good days.

15

In the Eye of the Storm

Five miles below Camp VIII and 800 miles to the south, a mass of warm, wet air churned inland from the Indian Ocean. For days to come, winds would push the warm air north through India and Pakistan until it ran against the high walls of the Himalaya and billowed upward. As the warm air rose, it would cool, condense, and transform into the worst monsoon storms the young nation of Pakistan had ever seen.

On the night of August 2, this roiling storm front slipped across the southern edge of the Himalaya and bore down on K2. At Camp VIII, the last climbers had just staggered up the snow slope and into camp. Molenaar celebrated their arrival in his diary that night. "Party again together!" he wrote. "Wonderful!"

The next morning, the sky was a sickly gray, and the wind blew with a vengeance. But Charlie Houston was feeling good. At this point on the mountain, Wiessner had been alone with Dudley Wolfe and Pasang Kikuli. Below him was a broken chain of debilitated teammates and frightened Sherpas. Houston, on the other hand, had made it to 25,000 feet with his party intact. Never before had an entire mountaineering team climbed this high.

The four tents at Camp VIII sat in a rectangle, doors facing the center. As the wind raged, the team managed to hold a conference and hatch a plan. Tomorrow, Tuesday, six climbers would move as high as they could and establish Camp IX. Two would stay there and try for the summit the next day. Meanwhile, four climbers would move back up from VIII with more supplies. A new party of two would stay and try for the summit on Thursday. On Friday, the entire team would head down the mountain, successful or not.

Molenaar listened to it all and couldn't help feeling nervous. The altitude had given him a splitting headache and a queasy stomach. The weather had been unpredictable at best, and their supplies wouldn't last forever. If they got a window of clear skies, shouldn't they use it to get off the mountain?

As he huddled with his diary that night, the tent snapping and pulling at its ropes, Molenaar worried that they were letting pride get in the way of good sense. His mind drifted to Seattle, 9,000 miles away, where the things he often found irritating suddenly seemed like a joy. What he wouldn't give right now to go shopping with Lee and Patti, to live "the wonderful life ahead in which no such material summits force one's pride and ego into battle, in which . . . it can be a real fine experience to realize that one needn't always be on top."

▲

That night, "the top" was the last thing on Charlie Houston's mind. He sat shoulder to shoulder with George Bell, praying they would survive the night. A violent gust of wind swept the tent and tore a small hole in the nylon wall. With the next onslaught, another rip appeared. Houston and Bell drifted in and out of sleep, the holes growing larger every time they opened their eyes. Bell was calm, as always, but it was terrifying how vulnerable they were— just a thin layer of nylon between them and a wind so fierce it could blow a man off his feet.

"Should we get out of the tent now and make a dash for the others?" Houston asked.

"I think we'll last till daylight," Bell said.

That was all they could hope. Finding boots and gathering gear in the dark seemed like more than they could handle. If they had to go out in the gale, even just to pile into another tent, Houston thought they might not survive. If the tent collapsed, they decided, they would huddle in the wreckage until the sun broke through.

Finally, around 7:00 a.m., the wind delivered its final

blow. The tent poles snapped in three places, and the nylon collapsed around them like a net.

"Our tent's gone!" they yelled.

Houston and Bell wriggled out of their sleeping bags and groped for their boots. When the wind let up for a moment, they crawled free of the tattered shelter and scrambled for the other tents. Houston dove in with Streather and Bates. Bell squeezed between Molenaar and Craig.

The tents already made a crowded home for two people. Now they would have to accommodate three. In Houston's tent, they could barely sit up. To Streather it felt like living under a cot with two other men.

For now, it was the only choice they had.

▲

For days, the wind and snow refused to let up. The Sherpas talked about the mountain as though it were a living spirit, and Bates now understood what they meant. Science was the tool he'd always used to understand nature, but out here, it was inadequate. The wind was so fierce that it seemed to blow with evil intent, as though they had awakened a spirit that was trying to blast them off the mountain.

During the worst spells, Bates, Streather, and Houston leaned on the windward side of the tent, trying to hold it down from the inside. After each brutal gust, they yelled to the next tent over: "Okay?!"

Looking west from Camp VIII, with the wreckage of Houston's tent at the lower left.

"Okay!" came the answer.

But no one was really okay. All the tents had gaps in them now, and the wind easily found a way in. They spent hours huddled around the stoves, trying to keep the flame from sputtering out. Most of the time, they failed. They went days without a hot meal and barely enough melted snow for a cup of tea. They survived on biscuits, jam, and meat bars.

In the meager shelter of the tents, they did what they could to keep themselves occupied. Bates read poetry to his tentmates. Houston fantasized out loud about his vacation spot beside a rippling lake in the Adirondack Mountains. Like prisoners planning their escape, they talked constantly about the summit. On August 5, they held a vote to pick the summit teams. As soon as they could climb, Craig and Bell would go first. Schoening and Gilkey would follow the next day.

When the weather allowed, Houston made his rounds from tent to tent, checking for signs of frostbite, trying to keep spirits high. Molenaar was always glad to see him. Somehow, in the face of it all, Houston stayed cheerful and energetic.

For Houston, there was one ritual he couldn't live without. Every day at 7:00 a.m. and 6:00 p.m., he dug in his sleeping bag where he kept the radio so its batteries wouldn't freeze. He clicked the button and spoke: "Hello

Base Camp, hello, Base Camp. This is Camp VIII. Can you hear me? Over."

Without fail, the cheerful voice of Colonel Ata-Ullah came back to him: "Hello, Charlie, I hear you very well. Give me your news, please. Over."

"Well, Ata, the storm keeps on up here. There is nothing to see, and we can't get out. But we are fighting-fit and ready to go. What is your news? Over."

Charlie could hear the reluctance in Ata's voice when he answered. The colonel was desperate to tell them something hopeful, but day after day the news was the same: Fresh snow at Base Camp, the peaks shrouded in dark clouds, more heavy snow and high winds forecast for 25,000 feet.

It wasn't what Charlie wanted to hear. But the sound of Ata's voice, scratching through the speaker, gave him strength. Somewhere beneath the clouds, there were other human beings waiting for them to come back to Earth.

▲

Thousands of miles away, in Seattle and Exeter and Iowa, Lee Molenaar, Dorcas Houston, and Art Gilkey's parents waited eagerly for news of the expedition. As far as they knew, the team was doing fine. Gilkey's parents had gotten letters from Art until he left Skardu. Since then, their only news came from the AAC, and it was usually two weeks old. The team wrote regular updates, but the letters had to be carried by runner to Askole before they started their journey across the ocean.

In July, a reporter from the *Des Moines Tribune* had asked Art's father if he worried about their son. "What's the use?" Herbert Gilkey said. "It's what the boy wants to do. His heart is so much in it, we couldn't want it otherwise. Of course, we know the hazards that are there . . . a glacial slide . . . a storm. But things can happen to you crossing the street, too."

On August 6, several papers ran small articles on the progress of the expedition. U.S. CLIMBERS MOVE UP K2, read a headline in the *Newport Daily News*. "Reports brought by runners said the team was in the best of health and spirits," the article claimed.

By the time the article appeared on the morning newsstands, darkness was falling over K2, half the world away. The climbers hadn't moved—up or down—in nearly a week. And their health could not be described as good.

Charlie Houston had made his rounds earlier in the day and discovered that George Bell and Dee Molenaar were done. Now, Bell lay in a sleeping bag, wiggling his toes to get feeling back in his feet. Already the flesh in two of his toes had begun to die. Black, gangrenous spots were spreading through his feet.

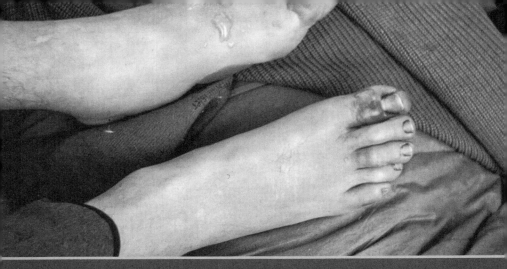

Bell's frostbitten toes.

Sandwiched in the tent next to Bell, Molenaar was also struggling with frostbite. He hadn't had much to eat or drink in days, and his throat hurt every time he swallowed. He and Bell were supposed to descend tomorrow if the weather allowed.

But the biggest blow to the fortunes of the Third American Karakoram Expedition was yet to come. In a few hours, as the sun lightened the sky over the mountain, Art Gilkey would collapse in the snow, and Houston would make another discovery: Gilkey had blood clots in his legs. The kid whose heart was so much in it that he had wanted more than any of them to stand at the top of K2 was going to die on the mountain if they could not get him down.

16

The Death Zone

O n the morning of August 7, Art Gilkey lay in his tent at Camp VIII, his leg wrapped in a bandage. Outside, the rest of the team held a hurried conference in the wind. Houston told them his grim diagnosis: Gilkey couldn't climb, and at 25,000 feet, he wasn't going to recover. Their mission had changed, he said. They were no longer trying to climb the mountain. They needed to get a sick man—and themselves—down alive.

A few hours ago, they had been hoping for weather calm enough to try for the summit. In fact, Gilkey had been chosen for the second summit team. Now, he couldn't even walk, and the rest of them could only hope the skies would clear long enough for them to start down the mountain.

Pete Schoening was ready for the new challenge. He thought they could get Gilkey down. He had rescued climbers on the steep slopes of the Cascade Mountains, and he knew it would be grueling, risky work. Frostbite would take its toll on all of them. But it could be done.

Houston didn't believe him. In fact, he didn't think Schoening believed himself. The steep ice slope just below them? The Black Pyramid? House's Chimney? It would take every bit of skill he had acquired in two decades of climbing, every ounce of strength he had left, just to get himself down the mountain. How could they possibly carry Art Gilkey down, too?

It was an impossible bind. They knew they would be risking seven lives in a probably useless attempt to save one. And yet, no one was willing to suggest the alternative. No one uttered the thought that since Art was likely to die anyway, he should be left behind. There would be no Dudley Wolfes on K2 this year.

And if there was no alternative, maybe it was better to think like Pete Schoening.

▲

For the first time in five days, they moved with real purpose. The clouds hung high in the sky and the wind had let up a little. Compared to lower altitudes it couldn't be called good weather, but they had to make use of it. Someone struck the smallest tent and packed it. Everyone rolled up their sleeping bags. They packed a couple of stoves and some food. Camp VI was fully stocked, but who could say for sure they would make it there by nightfall?

When everything was ready, they bundled Gilkey in a sleeping bag and wrapped him like a mummy in the remains of the collapsed tent. They secured him with ropes and started out down the snow slope toward the makeshift Camp VII.

Five days of monsoon storms had laid 2 to 3 feet of fresh snow on the slope. At first, they dragged Gilkey along, sinking to their hips. Then, as the slope steepened, they had to hold him back. The overcast turned to fog. They could barely see, but as they made their way through the loose snow, they realized what they should've known before they started. A week ago, when Schoening and Gilkey first set foot on the slope, it had been an avalanche risk. Now, with a fresh coating of unsettled snow, it was certain suicide. At any moment, the next step could dislodge hundreds of tons of snow and send them tumbling into free fall. They had to turn back.

No one had the strength to pull Gilkey back up the slope. He had to wriggle out of his cocoon to help. With Molenaar and Bell on either side, he balanced himself on his one good leg. He half hopped, half fell up the slope while they dragged him by the shoulders.

An hour and a half later, they staggered back into Camp VIII and repitched the tent they had taken down. They got Gilkey settled and crawled inside, depressed, exhausted, and trapped.

Gilkey at Camp VIII, no longer able to walk.

▲

The next morning brought a ray of hope. Schoening and Craig had scouted a new route along a rocky rim that bordered the right edge of the snow slope. The rim led to a gully that dropped to the level of the tiny Camp VII. The route was steep and icy, but it skirted the avalanche field. If they could lower Gilkey to the bottom of the gully, they could try to pull him like a pendulum across the ice slope to the camp.

After an hour spent wrestling with the stove for a few cups of tea, Houston paid a visit to Gilkey's tent and decided the patient looked better. The swelling in his leg was down a bit and he seemed to be in less pain. Gilkey looked up at him and said, "I'll be climbing again tomorrow."

It hurt to listen to him, still determined to get on his feet and climb the mountain. But who knows, Houston thought, maybe he was right. Houston made the rounds, and they all decided to wait another day to move. If they were lucky, the weather would improve and Gilkey would be able to help get himself down. The chance was slim, but at this point, they would take anything. According to Molenaar, they were all losing strength fast. "Our present battle," he wrote, "is against altitude-caused deterioration and against the constant threat of frostbite."

The entire team had been at 25,000 feet for more than a week. No one had been that high for that long, and doctors were just beginning to understand the risks. The headaches climbers get lower on the mountain can turn into cerebral edema, in which pressure builds around the brain. That pressure can scramble the brain's signals to the limbs. More common is pulmonary edema, in which the lungs fill with fluid and can drown a climber in a matter of hours. In both cases, the only cure is to descend. Fast.

Just that year, the Swiss doctor Wyss-Dunant had invented the term Death Zone to describe what happens to human life at extreme altitudes. "*Survival* is the only term suitable for describing the behavior of a man in that mortal zone," Wyss-Dunant wrote. "Life hangs by a thread, to such a point that the organism, exhausted by the ascent, can pass in a few hours from a somnolent state to a white death . . . It is now no longer a question of adaptation, but only of the number of days or hours allotted to the strongest person."

Dee Molenaar had no idea how many days or hours they each had left. But he began to have a disturbing thought: If the time came when he had to climb or die, would he have the willpower to act? He could feel the altitude wearing away his desire to get out of the tent in the morning. It was partly physical—just to sit up and light a stove made his heart race and his lungs heave. But it was mental, too.

Trapped in the tents at 25,000 feet, he suddenly understood the final days of Dudley Wolfe's life, played out somewhere on the ice slope just below their camp. He could imagine seeing Kikuli, Phinsoo, and Kitar at the tent door, and knowing somewhere deep inside that if he didn't get out of his sleeping bag, find his boots, and descend with them, he would die alone, 9,000 miles from home. He could imagine knowing all of this and still saying to himself, *I prefer not. Instead, I will pull my sleeping bag tight under my chin and stay right here.*

▲

The next day, Houston poked his head into the tent where Molenaar, Bell, and Craig lay shoulder to shoulder. He crawled in, bringing a spray of fine white powder with him. Outside, the wind howled and snow came down in solid sheets of white.

Houston asked how they were feeling—then he delivered the bad news. He had just come from Gilkey's tent. During the night, Art had developed a dry, hacking cough, and when Houston listened to Gilkey's breathing, his heart sank. At least two blood clots had passed into Gilkey's lungs. At this altitude, he didn't have long to live. They would have to get him down first thing tomorrow.

Tears welled up in Molenaar's eyes. He hadn't gotten to know Art as well as he would have liked. Gilkey was quiet and serious. And if Molenaar was the voice of caution on the expedition, Gilkey was his foil—always a vote for pushing higher. But Art was a hardworking teammate, eager to carry loads and pitch tents. His desire to climb was pure. It was hard to bear, listening to him cough in the next tent, knowing he probably wouldn't make it down alive.

But with that thought, Molenaar let his mind drift to another place—a place the others had surely gone as well. "Terrible thought that perhaps our getting down safely depends on Art's early passing," he wrote. "Oh God, save me from such thoughts!"

Later, Molenaar sat down to write what he thought might be his last letter to Lee. It was August 9, Patti's birthday. "The situation right now looks as desperate as any I've ever experienced," he began.

He talked about each of his teammates and the bond they'd developed since leaving New York so many weeks ago. "We all feel strong obligations to each other, depend so much on each other that there's no thought of 'every man for himself' in this desperate plight," he wrote. "We all come down or else."

The "or else" sounded so final it sent him spiraling into despair. He felt like a "condemned man," thinking about Lee and Patti waiting for him back in Seattle. He was praying for the strength to make it down alive. "How I wish I was with you & Patti, our lovely little girl, who I want so much to be with more, and still hope to—"

That brought him up short, and he wrote one final line: "God, what a depressing letter—an obituary or something, which I certainly don't plan on yet! We have so much to live for!"

▲

All the praying and hoping for three clear days had gotten them nothing. August 10 was as bad as any day they'd seen on the mountain, the wind raging and snow blowing sideways through the air. But today, they had no choice. Food and fuel was almost gone. Gilkey was dying. They had to get off the mountain.

They repeated the preparations of three days ago—tents struck, sleeping bags packed, Gilkey wrapped tight. He looked warm, bundled inside a sleeping bag and a tent, his feet stuffed in a rucksack.

Houston had moved in with Gilkey the day before and given him morphine for the pain. In the tent, Gilkey was as eager as ever. He apologized for burdening everyone. As soon as they got him down, he told Houston, the rest of the team should make another try for the summit.

Now, as they wrapped Gilkey in his cocoon, someone asked, "How are you?"

"Just fine—just fine," he said.

With everything packed, Houston made a final call to Ata. "It's pretty desperate," he reported, "but we can't wait. We're starting down now. We'll call you at 3 o'clock."

In the driving snow, they left the remains of their camp behind. Molenaar and Schoening went ahead to scout the route, hugging the rock rim on the right. Bates and Houston stayed high, anchored to Gilkey by a rope. Slowly they lowered the cocoon down the slope. Craig descended alongside Gilkey, guiding him through the snow and shouting instructions up the mountain. Streather, with Bell belaying him from above, climbed halfway down so he could relay messages above the deafening sound of the wind.

For a couple of hours they moved this way, the wind biting through jackets and gloves. They found the rock rim and headed down along its edge. Houston and Bates dug themselves into the slope with the ropes wrapped around their hips. Slowly, they paid out rope, lowering

Gilkey 120 feet until the slack ran out. Then they climbed down one by one, keeping Art anchored until they could start again down the narrow gully of snow.

They had reached the steepest pitch when Streather, from his perch in the middle, saw the ropes scrape the fresh snow above Craig and Gilkey. Just as he started to yell a warning, the snow loosened and avalanched down the slope. Craig and Gilkey disappeared in a white cloud.

Above the avalanche, Houston and Bates felt the rope tighten. They leaned back into the slope and gripped the rope with frostnipped hands. Everything below vanished.

Then they heard Streather yell up to them: "Hold him! He's on the edge of a cliff."

▲

For just a moment, as the avalanche rumbled off down the mountain and the snow spray cleared, there was no movement on the high southern edge of K2. Bob Craig clung to one of the ropes attached to Art Gilkey's cocoon. He had reacted quickly when the ground began to shift under his boots. He grabbed for the rope and hung on while the powdery slide tried to tear him off the mountain. Now, he and Gilkey lay perched at the top of a steep, rocky cliff.

One hundred feet above the two men, Houston and Bates hugged the slope, crampons and ice axes dug deep in the snow. They had done their job and held the belay. Gilkey was still there, tethered to the ropes that bit into their waists.

Houston, Bates, and Streather ready to descend with Gilkey wrapped in his cocoon.

George Bell stood near Houston and Bates, his feet nearly frozen solid. At the end of his rope, halfway to Gilkey's cocoon, Tony Streather leaned on his ice axe, surprised to see Craig emerge from the remnants of the avalanche.

Below Craig and Gilkey and halfway across the ice slope to the site of Camp VII, Schoening and Molenaar were the first to move. They traversed carefully over to the cocoon and asked Gilkey how he was doing.

"Just fine," he said. "Just fine."

Bob Craig, however, was spent. He was shivering, gasping for breath, and could barely lift his arms. Molenaar got him on a short rope and set off across the ice slope to the camp so Craig could rest.

Meanwhile, Schoening anchored Gilkey to a solid belay. He jammed the handle of his ice axe into the snow just above a rock that had frozen into the slope. He wrapped one of Gilkey's ropes around his waist and then around the axe. Once he had a belay established, they lowered Gilkey carefully down the rocky cliff, with Streather guiding the cocoon. Houston and Bates, finally freed from their frigid perch, climbed down to join the rest.

Once they had Gilkey at the level of Camp VII, they had to pull him across the ice slope to the tiny ledge. From there, they could rest and figure out how to negotiate the Black Pyramid.

Houston and Bates, still roped together, traversed toward the camp, trying to find a place to anchor to the slope so they could pull Gilkey with them. Molenaar came back up to help, tied himself to the cocoon, and started moving toward the camp. Streather, still anchored to Bell, had a last word with Gilkey and came over to help Molenaar. From there, Streather looked up the slope at Bell, who was starting down to join them.

To Streather, Bell looked shaky. His frozen feet weren't

Molenaar later drew this sketch of Schoening digging in to belay Gilkey.

carrying him the way they should. His hands looked as useless as clubs. Streather saw him clutch at a handhold and then slip. As someone shouted above the roar of the wind, Bell began to slide down the slope, swiping at the ice with his axe. He careened past Streather, picking up speed as he went. Streather dug his crampons in a little deeper, clung to his axe, and waited for the rope to go taut.

17

The Fall

Later, George Bell would remember what he felt during the fall: absolutely nothing.

It was like that for all of them. There was no room for terror and no hope of survival. They had spent weeks fighting their way up the mountain, defying gravity by force of will. Now, sliding down the ice slope, there was nothing they could do. Years later, the climber Joe Simpson would survive a 150-foot fall in the Andes Mountains and describe the experience this way: "The violent and numbing reality of plunging down a mountainside is in fact so brutal that there is no time for fear. More often than not it is an experience of deep calm resignation, an utter helplessness so profound that knowing we can do nothing leaves us emotionally empty."

▲

Tony Streather was the first to be yanked off his perch. He watched Bell rocket past him, heard a yell, felt a jerk around his waist, and plunged into free fall. He felt another tug and stopped for a second before lurching down the slope again.

Dee Molenaar squinted into the whirling snow and saw Bell sliding down the slope past Gilkey's cocoon. "Goddamn, there goes Bell!" he yelled. An instant later, Molenaar was facedown on the ice and skidding down the mountain. Rock slabs flew past and the rim of the Black Pyramid loomed below and he knew that in a second a blow to the head would knock him out and that would be the end of it. But in the moment, there were no thoughts of Lee and Patti, no memories of his family flashing before his eyes. There was only the exhilaration of giving in to gravity. It felt like he was flying.

Bob Bates didn't see Molenaar fall, but it looked to him like an invisible hand was swatting people off the slope—first Streather, then Houston—and Houston was roped to him! Bates swung his ice axe wildly at the slope, but when the rope went taut, Houston's weight flipped him backward off the ice. He landed on his pack and slid head-first down the mountain, the hood of his parka pulled over his eyes. Down he went, bumping over rocks embedded in the ice, feeling an eerie distance from it all. It was over, he thought, and there wasn't a thing he could do about it. He had lived a good life, climbed well, and now it was done.

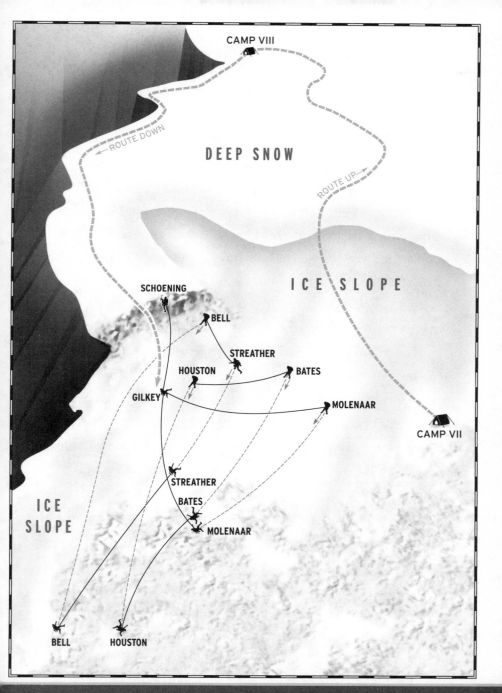

CAMP VIII

ROUTE DOWN

DEEP SNOW

ROUTE UP

ICE SLOPE

SCHOENING

BELL

STREATHER

HOUSTON

BATES

GILKEY

MOLENAAR

CAMP VII

STREATHER

BATES

MOLENAAR

ICE
SLOPE

BELL

HOUSTON

The scene of the fall, based on a drawing by Molenaar.

Then, with a sharp tug of the rope around his waist, he stopped.

They all stopped.

▲

High on the slope, at the top of a rat's nest of taut and tangled ropes, Pete Schoening leaned against his ice axe, a single rope carving into his hips. It had all happened in seconds. He saw George Bell start to go and braced himself in case Bell's rope got caught in his own. The impact came in a series of jolts—the rope tightening around his waist, the axe straining against the rock that held it in place.

The jolts stopped and left the rope quivering, stretched to half its normal width. Schoening gripped it hard and leaned into the axe, trying to take weight off the rock. If the rock broke free of the ice, there was no way the belay would hold. Gilkey and whoever else he was holding would go tumbling down the mountainside—and he would go with them.

Schoening was afraid to turn around. He could tell his belay was supporting a lot more than just Art Gilkey's cocoon. Had he been able to take in the entire slope below, he would have pieced together what happened: One rope swept into another and then another, pulling five climbers into free fall down the mountain. Now, those five men and Art Gilkey's cocoon lay tangled in a web of ropes on a sheer ice slope, saved from an 8,000-foot fall to the

Godwin-Austen Glacier by Schoening and his axe.

Pete Schoening didn't know all of this. But he did know that the wind was howling and his hands were freezing and the rope had been stretched near its breaking point. Below him, he heard Tony Streather yell to anyone who could hear him, "Get your weight off the rope!"

▲

At least 200 feet below Schoening, Bates lay splayed on his back with his head below his feet. His arms were hopelessly tangled in a web of rope over his head. He tried to move and couldn't, which was just as well. He had stopped at the edge of a steep drop-off near the top of the Black Pyramid, his head nearly hanging off the ledge.

He heard a groan come from surprisingly close, and then a voice.

"Who's there?" someone asked.

Bates looked up to see Molenaar picking himself up off the slope, blood dripping from his nose onto his beard. Molenaar was shaken from the fall, but he managed to free Bates's arms from the rope. They both got a better purchase on the ledge and began to look around.

Fifty feet up the slope, Streather stood on shaky legs, trying to make sense of the tangle of ropes around his waist. Seventy-five feet below, Bell was hauling himself over a ledge that seemed to drop off into nothing. To Bell's right, a crumpled figure lay on a ledge below a 30-foot cliff. The figure was Charlie Houston, and he wasn't moving at all.

As Bell climbed closer through the blowing snow, Bates could see he had lost his backpack, his goggles, and his gloves. "My hands are freezing," Bell said. Bates pulled out a spare pair of mittens and handed his backpack off to Molenaar. His sleeping bag had nearly been torn loose during the fall, and tonight it could mean the difference between life and death. He climbed down to Bell, whose hands and face had turned a sickly white. He wrestled the mittens onto Bell's frozen hands and scrambled as quickly as he could over to Houston.

Houston lay unconscious on the ledge, and Bates leaned over him, expecting the worst. But when he touched a shoulder, Charlie's eyes opened. Houston propped himself up and tried to focus on the surroundings. "Where are we?" he asked. "What are we doing here?"

Bates explained exactly why they were clinging to the side of a 28,000-foot mountain in a blizzard. Then, while Molenaar anchored Houston's rope from above, Bates tried to get his friend to climb. Again and again, he told Houston they had to get to shelter, but Houston wouldn't budge. He had obviously suffered a concussion, and his eyes wouldn't focus. It was like talking to a sleepwalker.

Bates started to grow desperate. They had all survived the fall, but in their current state they couldn't possibly haul Houston up 150 feet of steep rock and ice to camp.

Finally, Bates grabbed his friend and looked him in the eye. "Charlie," he said, "if you ever want to see Dorcas and Penny again, climb up there right *now!*"

Houston suddenly looked terrified. He said nothing, turned, and scrambled up the slope to Molenaar. As Bates climbed up after him, he could hear Charlie asking Molenaar, "What are we doing here?"

▲

When George Bell lost his footing at the top of the ice slope, Bob Craig had been at Camp VII, recovering from the avalanche and trying to get a tent set up on the tiny ledge. He heard a couple of shouts and looked up. A moment ago, the team had been stretched out across 150 feet of ice slope, trying to pull Art Gilkey across to the camp. Suddenly they had vanished. All he could make out was a single ice axe, jammed into the slope. Then a curtain of swirling snow came down and obscured it all.

Craig summoned whatever strength he had left and crossed the slope, relieved to see Bates, Molenaar, and Houston making their way to the camp. He found his way to Gilkey, who claimed he was still doing fine.

Sixty feet up the slope, Pete Schoening had been dug in with his rock and his ice axe for what seemed like hours. His burden had lightened since the walking wounded had untangled themselves from the ropes. But he couldn't wait to move. His fingers felt like icicles, and he had no protection from the wind. He watched while Streather and Craig anchored Gilkey's cocoon to two ice axes, driven deep in the snow. Finally, he felt his own rope slacken. He willed his stiffened limbs to life and climbed to Camp VII.

Craig finished securing Gilkey to the slope. He explained to Art that everyone had survived the fall, but Bell, Molenaar, and Houston were in pretty bad shape. They needed to get the injured settled at Camp VII and carve out another platform so they could all squeeze into two tents for the night. They'd be back in an hour at the most, Craig promised.

Then he said goodbye to Gilkey.

▲

At Camp VII, seven men shuffled in an exhausted daze around a slope as steep as a roof. They were grateful to be alive, but no one was celebrating. They simply wanted to survive another night.

While the snow blew in great gusts across the slope, they wrestled a two-man tent into place on the tiny platform that Schoening and Gilkey had carved out of the ice nearly two weeks before. They anchored the tent with rocks and then pitons, the wind trying all the while to carry it off like a kite. With the thin nylon flapping in the gale, Houston, Molenaar, Bell, and Schoening climbed inside. Schoening was desperate to warm his frosted hands. Houston was still reeling from his head injury. Molenaar had cracked a rib in

Pete at Camp VII nearly two weeks earlier, setting up the one-person tent that would now have to shelter three for at least one night.

the fall, and he had nasty gashes in his thigh and above his nose. Bell's feet were frozen and fast becoming useless. No one wanted to think about the prospect of getting more disabled climbers down the mountain.

While the wounded huddled together out of the wind, Bates, Craig, and Streather hacked another platform out of the ice. They needed a space just big enough for the small tent Schoening and Gilkey had stayed in on the way up. The tent was made to shelter one person; somehow they would have to pack three into it tonight. While they worked, they thought they could hear Gilkey shouting through the howl of the wind.

The three men finished as fast as they could and roped up to traverse the ice slope. They knew they didn't have the strength to drag Gilkey back to camp, but they thought they could carve a cave in the snow big enough to protect him for the night.

Bates and Streather took the lead, squinting into the blowing snow. After a few minutes, Bates stopped. This must have been the place where they anchored Gilkey, and yet there was nothing but bare slope. He turned back to Streather.

"Art's gone," he said.

Streather climbed past Bates and found the groove in the snow where he was certain they had left the cocoon. It looked different, somehow. The texture of the snow had changed. A rock he had noticed before wasn't there anymore. It looked like an avalanche had rumbled down the slope, pulled Gilkey from the anchors, and swept him down the mountain.

The three men looked down the slope, hoping to see a rope caught on a rock and Gilkey's cigar-shaped form resting beneath it. They yelled his name a few times, but they knew it was useless.

It was hard to get their minds around. Just an hour ago, Gilkey had been lying there, bundled in his cocoon, telling Streather he was "fine, just fine." Now he was gone.

"It was as if the hand of God had swept him away," Bates would later say.

For years, Art Gilkey had lived to climb. He had chosen

work that would take him back to the mountains again and again. His heart was so much in it that his parents had resigned themselves to the risks he took.

Near the end, when Houston moved into his tent to care for him, Gilkey refused to admit that the mountain had beaten them. But he had let his guard down the night before with Pete Schoening, the youngest member of the team. Lying in his sleeping bag, as high above the oceans as he would ever climb, he had said to Pete, "There's no better place to die than K2."

18

Fellowship of the Rope

t some point in the night, the wind died, as though a whimsical god decided they'd suffered enough for now. But in the two tiny tents, wedged into the mountainside at 24,000 feet, no one felt secure.

Schoening, Craig, and Streather had stuffed themselves inside the one-person tent. They sat shoulder to shoulder with their backs against the ice slope, afraid to move around. At their feet, a third of the tent hung over the ledge. A little more weight on that end and the tent would slip off the edge and carry them with it—if an avalanche didn't do the job first. Hundreds of tons of fresh snow still covered the slope above their heads, poised to rumble down the mountain at any time.

In the larger tent, they had another hazard to contend with: Charlie Houston. Houston and Bates sat wedged between Bell and Molenaar. A single air mattress gave them some insulation from the cold. Bates had wrapped a sleeping bag around their legs, and Molenaar insisted on giving his down jacket to Houston to keep him warm. But as the night wore on, it wasn't Houston's body temperature they worried about. It was his mind.

Houston seemed to be grasping what had happened to them, but it didn't bring him much comfort. He spent the first part of the night worrying in turn about anyone he couldn't see.

"How's Pete?" he would ask.

"He's fine," Bates would answer.

Not convinced that Bates was an authority on the subject, Houston would ask again.

Finally, Bates would call out to the other tent, "Hey, Pete, tell Charlie you're all right."

"I'm fine, Charlie," Pete would say. "Don't worry about me."

That would buy a minute or two of silence until they'd hear, "How's Tony?"

Eventually, Houston's own struggles distracted him. He had bruised a rib in the fall, and every breath sent a stab of pain through his chest. But he decided his breathing problems had nothing to do with his body. He kept reaching up to tear a hole in the tent, insisting they needed more oxygen. Molenaar finally opened the tent door, but even that didn't satisfy Houston.

"I know about these things," Houston said urgently. "I

have studied them. We'll all be dead in three minutes if you don't let me cut a hole in the tent."

▲

The next morning, seven men emerged onto the slope, having breathed well enough to make it through the night. They had barely slept and they were battered from the fall, but there was work to do. They struck the tents and gathered their gear. The wind had returned, and as they peered down toward Camp VI, the jagged rocks of the Black Pyramid faded into a dense fog. But there was no discussion of the weather and no debate over whether or not to climb today. They needed to get down the mountain before frostbite or altitude sickness crippled them all.

The question for the day was whether Houston and Bell could negotiate the Black Pyramid under their own power. Bell's feet were so swollen it took a couple of people to get them into his boots. To make matters worse, he had lost his glasses in the fall. Even if his feet would support him, he could barely see where to put them. As for Houston, no one knew what to expect. Maybe his years of climbing experience would take over and guide him down the mountain. If not, he could be a danger to anyone climbing with him.

Schoening and Craig, the two strongest climbers, tied Houston between them and started down the mountain. Great sheets of snow spray whipped at their hands as they grappled for holds. Not far into the climb, Houston sat down on a ledge. He looked around as though once again it took a supreme effort to figure out how he had been plucked from his medical practice in Exeter, New Hampshire, and deposited on a mountainside in Asia. From above, Schoening shook the rope and told him to get moving. Houston picked himself up and climbed.

Above them, Bates, Bell, Molenaar, and Streather climbed roped together. They took turns stopping to belay one another—clipped into a piton, or clinging to an ice ax jammed into a patch of crusty snow. But no one had much faith that he would be able to stop a fall. Bell's hands and feet were barely functional. Molenaar's injured leg throbbed when he took a step, and his ribs made it painful to reach.

On the way down, they spotted Houston's ice axe, lying on an outcropping of rock. Molenaar traversed to get it and handed it to Bell, who had lost his in the fall. Bates watched from above as Bell picked his way down, leaning danger-ously out over the slope to tap the rock with the axe like a blind man.

By midafternoon, Schoening and Craig had guided Houston to the final pitch above Camp VI. As they neared the camp, a solemn sight came into view. Pete Schoening paused for a moment and looked to his left. About 1,000 feet below the spot where he had held Art Gilkey fast to the mountainside, a sleeping bag dangled from a ledge, swinging empty in the wind. Below it, for 500 feet or so, the rocks were stained with blood.

They passed the pitch without much said. Not long after, Streather, Bell, Molenaar, and Bates reached the same spot. Bell could barely stand, and Molenaar felt nearly hysterical from weakness. Still, the evidence of Gilkey's last moments had a deep impact on them all. It would be a long time before they could talk about it. They were painfully aware that Gilkey's death had probably saved them, but that didn't make it easier to stomach. Bates told himself that Gilkey had been knocked unconscious on the rocks and hadn't suffered during the fall.

In the relative comfort of Camp VI that night, Molenaar recorded in his diary: "Poor Art!"

▲

By 6:00 p.m., they had dug out the tents and settled in at Camp VI. Someone worked the stove, putting together a feast of rice, tomato soup, canned ham, and tea. Then they dug up a radio they had left in camp. They had lost the other one in the fall and hadn't called Ata-Ullah in more than a day and a half. Houston was lucid enough to make the call.

"Thank god," Ata said when he heard Houston's voice.

Since 3:00 p.m. the day before, Ata-Ullah had been sitting by his radio waiting for a call. He'd been planning to search the glacier the next day for evidence of an

Packing up to descend on August 11, with the slope they came down the day before visible in the upper right.

avalanche. As soon as the weather broke, he was going to climb as high as he could to look for them. But he had convinced himself they were probably dead.

The next day, Schoening and Streather descended ahead to Camp V and made tea for the others. By nightfall, the rest of the team still hadn't arrived. The wind had picked up at Camp VI, and it was bitter cold. They decided they couldn't risk Bell's feet by climbing. And Bob Craig was showing signs of bad frostbite as well. They would take a rest day and hope for better weather tomorrow.

Finally, on August 13, three days after they had started down with Gilkey's cocoon, the entire team stumbled down the mountain to House's Chimney. A month ago, on the way up, it had taken them five minutes to descend from Camp V to the top of the Chimney. Now, on the edge of total exhaustion, it took them an hour.

One by one, they rappelled down the 80-foot groove in the cliff. Houston, who was feeling better but still recovering from his concussion, insisted on belaying everyone from the top. He dug in, wrapped the rope around his hips, and lowered his teammates slowly down the cliff. After each man went a backpack. It was slow, painstaking work, and by the time Bob Bates swung out over the edge and climbed down, it was nearly dark.

Charlie Houston stood alone at the top of House's Chimney. On the way up the mountain, this had been the site of his triumph. He had sat on the ledge after leading the climb with half the Karakoram laid out beneath him, feeling like he belonged on this mountain, like he had unlocked the gate to the summit of K2.

It was just over a month ago, but it might as well have been 20 years.

Now, he peered down the chimney, flooded with doubt. Below him hung not just the rope he needed but old, rotten ropes from '38 and '39. What if he picked the wrong rope? What if he made a mistake on the way down? He could fall on Schoening, who was waiting at the base of the chimney to lead him into Camp IV. He could break a leg and become yet another burden to the team.

The thought occurred to him that he should just jump. For a moment he stood on the edge of the 80-foot cliff, still in a fog from his concussion. Just a step or two forward, and he would have joined Art Gilkey, Dudley Wolfe, and Pasang Kikuli, entombed on the Abruzzi Ridge for centuries to come.

Then, from 80 feet away, he could hear Schoening and maybe the others yelling at him to come down. He mumbled the Lord's Prayer into the wind and lowered himself off the side.

When Pete Schoening welcomed Houston at the base of House's Chimney, he had no idea how close the team had come to another tragedy. For Houston, the moment had passed. He climbed into a tent at Camp IV with Bates and Molenaar, knowing they were almost off the mountain. Tomorrow they would have to cut Bell's boots to make them fit his swollen feet. But they had escaped the worst that K2 had to offer. They would all get home alive.

▲

After 6:00 p.m. the next day, the men stood at the top of a steep gully looking down at the tents of Camp II. It had taken them 10 hours to make their way down from Camp IV. With the light dimming over the mountain, they heard a sound that filled them with emotion. The Hunza porters had caught sight of them and stood below, shouting with joy up the slope. Ghulam, Vilyati, and Hidayat quickly roped up and started climbing. When they reached the exhausted group, the porters were sobbing. They hugged each of the climbers and lifted the packs from their backs.

When they staggered into camp below, the Americans sat on sleeping bags that had been laid out on the rocks for

Houston and Molenaar with porters at Camp II.

them. The Hunzas, still weeping, pulled off their boots and fixed them rice and tea. For the first time in weeks, stars hung in the sky over the mountain. At one point, Kairal Hidayat led the Hunzas in a Muslim prayer for Gilkey.

It was a moving experience for Bates and the others. For days, their lives had hung on their own skill and effort—laboring to get the stove lit so they wouldn't die of thirst, willing themselves to the next handhold and the next. Now, they gave themselves over to the Hunzas, who cared for them as though they were sick children. It seemed a profound thing to see such kindness and compassion stretched across languages and cultures. And so, together, they sat under the stars and cried.

"It's the deepest experience I've ever had with a human being," Bob Craig would remember a couple of days later at Base Camp.

▲

On August 16, the Hunzas collected rocks from the glacier around Base Camp and stacked them in a 10-foot tower under the shadow of K2. George Bell and Bob Craig, who could no longer walk, watched from the tents while everyone else gathered around the somber gray cairn. Earlier, they had packed Gilkey's personal belongings to be carried out and sent home to his parents. Now, they placed a poem and a letter in a small metal box with Gilkey's name on it and set it on the cairn. Bob Bates said a prayer. Then they

His feet ravaged by frostbite, Bell is helped back to Base Camp by two porters.

went back to the tents to get ready for the trek to Askole and Skardu and, finally, the voyage home.

Art Gilkey was gone, but as the rest of them packed stoves and sleeping bags, tents and ropes, they knew they would be a part of each other's lives for a long time to come. "We started as strangers," Houston would later say, "but we came down the mountain as brothers." They hadn't reached the summit, but they had forged the bond that Houston talked about—the fellowship of the rope. On the ice slope near Camp VII, the half-inch strands of woven nylon that bound them together had nearly turned one

Bates (first to the right of the cairn) leads a service for Gilkey in front of the cairn built by the porters.

man's slip into certain death for the rest of them. Then, with the help of Pete Schoening and his ice axe, the ropes had saved them all.

The next day, a procession of climbers and porters made their way down the Godwin-Austen Glacier. Bob Craig limped along under his own power. Several porters carried George Bell, wrapped in a sleeping bag and strapped to a stretcher. Art Gilkey's body lay behind them somewhere on the slopes of K2, the mountain that had been there for millions of years before they tried to climb it and would be there for millions of years after they were gone.

EPILOGUE

A Beautiful Failure

By September, the surviving members of the Third American Karakoram Expedition had all come home. Pete Schoening married his fiancée, Mell Deuter, less than two weeks after he arrived in Seattle. Dee Molenaar finally got to see his wife, Lee, and his daughter, Patti. But on the way home from the airport, Lee told him she wanted a divorce. The letter he had composed to her the day before they left Camp VIII stayed where he had written it, bound in his diary.

Over the Christmas holidays, Bob Bates went off to spend three days with Art Gilkey's parents in Iowa. By that time, the Gilkeys had long held a letter from Houston, explaining the details of their son's last days. The letter assured them that Art had died quickly in the end. It failed to mention the bloody rocks they had seen above Camp VI.

Houston concluded this way: "Nothing I can tell you will help, I am afraid, but I can say that no group of people have

Porters carried Bell during the entire trek from K2 back to Skardu.

ever come closer together in toil and danger than have we. Art was a splendid man and closer to us than many families."

The two members of the expedition "family" who suffered most on the way down the mountain—Bob Craig and George Bell—recovered almost fully. Craig had no lasting effects from his frostbite. Bell arrived home on a stretcher. At Massachusetts General Hospital, they managed to save everything except two toes.

On the way back to the United States, Bell had been asked by reporters to describe K2. "It's a savage mountain," he said from his stretcher. "It tries to kill you."

▲

If K2 really was defending its slopes with evil intent, it failed to scare Charlie Houston. Before he left India, he was already telling reporters he would come back to take on the mountain again.

Back in New Hampshire, Houston reunited with his kids, settled into his work as a doctor, and secured a permit to climb K2 in 1955. Then, on August 4, 1954, he got a message that sent his life veering in another direction. Five days earlier, exactly a year after Schoening and Gilkey reached the site of their highest camp, two members of an Italian expedition had climbed the rocks where Pasang Lama made his evening ultimatum to Fritz Wiessner, slipped past the giant overhanging serac, slogged up the final snow slope, and stood on the summit of K2.

Houston was devastated. He sat down and wrote to a friend, "There are other hills, other interests, but K2 has filled my heart and head for sixteen years . . . Nothing can replace them, no second ascents, no other mountains . . . That phase of my life is over. Perhaps I shall grow up, but right now I feel that I have grown down."

The next day, Houston went off by himself on an errand to Nashua, New Hampshire, about 40 miles away from home. By the time he got there, he had no idea who he was. He did not remember nearly reaching the summit of Nanda Devi or losing Art Gilkey on K2. He did not know he had a wife and three kids and a medical practice in Exeter. He had lost every shred of his memory.

Somehow, Houston found his way to a hospital in Nashua, disoriented and distraught. A policeman noticed a label on his tie from a shop in Exeter, and after a couple of phone calls, Dorcas appeared at the hospital to bring Charlie home.

No one could explain why Houston lost his memory, but within 24 hours it came back. With it came the ghosts of his ordeal on K2. When he left for a family vacation in the Adirondacks a few days later, the scene of Gilkey's final moments on the rocks above Camp VI haunted him. The sight of the blood and the dangling sleeping bag had been too painful to talk about, even with his climbing partners.

Now, as he drove the back roads of Vermont and New York, he imagined he saw splotches of blood leaking through the pavement, just like the stained rocks on K2.

Charlie Houston never climbed again.

▲

The members of the Third American Karakoram Expedition stayed friends for the rest of their lives. They exchanged letters. They got together for reunions. In 1958, Pete Schoening returned to the Himalaya to climb the 26,510-foot peak, Gasherbrum I. On the way back he detoured past K2 and stood for a while at the base of Art Gilkey's cairn.

Since then, the 10-foot-tall pile of stones has become a monument to all the climbers who have lost their lives on K2. It's covered in metal plaques that jingle in the wind, each of them a testament to someone who decided, as a young Charlie Houston once wrote, "to take risks . . . [rather] than die within from rot."

None of the plaques tell a story as iconic as the one the cairn was built to commemorate. Over the years, the effort made to save Art Gilkey has become for many people a model of heroism in the mountains. Pete Schoening's ice axe is famous among climbers for its role in the belay that saved six men. It sits on display at the American Alpine Club Library in Golden, Colorado. The story of the climb is told again and again on anniversaries of the expedition. "It is now one of the great legends of the mountains," wrote the British climber Jim Curran. "In the annals of Himalayan climbing, there is nothing finer than this."

Charlie Houston and the others didn't see themselves as heroes. Houston was racked with guilt over losing Art Gilkey, and it was a big reason why he quit climbing for good. "As the prime mover for the expedition and the doctor I had failed," he wrote later. "We did not reach the summit, and I had been unable to save our friend's life. That our peers praise us for actions we saw implicit in the mountain spirit is irrelevant."

What exactly is this "mountain spirit" that was so important to Houston? The day before he suffered his attack of amnesia, he wrote a letter to the *New York Times* about the Italian expedition. He praised them for their "courage and their perseverance." But he also lamented the fact that the Italians had conquered the mountain with a military-like expedition. Five hundred porters lugged 10 tons of supplies to the mountain for them. Included in the loads were 230 oxygen tanks. The leader of the expedition, Ardito Desio, even flew around the mountain in a plane to scout their route.

To Houston, the Italians had accomplished the goal but left the experience itself empty. "I hope more climbers will make expeditions for the love of climbing, rather than for pride of conquest," he wrote. "I would not deny that the summit matters and matters greatly, but I know that the rewards of climbing live in the venture and not alone in the triumph. It is the means which calls us to the end, not the end which justifies the means. Climbers, all men indeed, will be more rewarded by their exertions if freed from the compulsion to win."

As a group, climbers tend to be ambitious, driven people. At some point on some mountain, most of them have to weigh their ambition to summit against the risk of pushing forward, their competitive drive against a commitment to their tentmates.

In 1939, Fritz Wiessner climbed on K2 possessed by the desire to conquer the mountain. Somewhere on the slopes, Wiessner, Durrance, Wolfe, and the rest of the expedition lost touch with one another. They climbed roped together, but the bond was purely physical. In the end, four lives were lost and nothing was won. In 1953, Dee Molenaar was humbled by K2. Stuck in the storm at 25,000 feet, he decided he didn't need the summit. He found a way to accept defeat without a "blow to the ego or pride." On the way down, during the brutal night at Camp VII, he took off his jacket and draped it over the injured Charlie Houston.

Houston's expedition didn't reach the top of K2. They lost Art Gilkey on the way down. But they discovered something more important than the summit of the world's second-highest peak. According to the Italian climber Reinhold Messner, "They failed in the most beautiful way you can imagine."

Pete Schoening, back at the mountain in 1958, gazes up at the summit, the site of their fall barely visible at the upper right.

Pitons with metal clips known as carabiners. Climbers clipped carabiners into the pitons and ran ropes through the carabiners to create protection on the mountain.

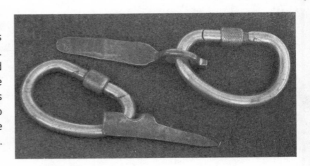

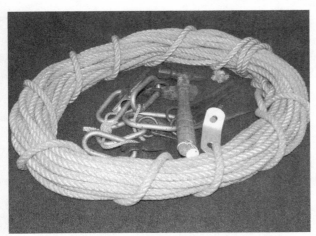

Mountaineers carried coils of rope in 100- or 120-foot lengths. In 1938, Houston and his team brought a total of 1,700 feet to K2.

Crampons were clunky contraptions that strapped to the bottom of climbing boots for traction on the ice.

A hammer used to pound pitons into tiny cracks in the rock face.

The Gear

The climbers in this book entrusted their lives to their equipment. Here's a look at the kind of gear Houston and his team would have used on K2 in the 1950s.

The famous ice axe that Pete Schoening used to save his climbing partners in 1953. It's now on display at the American Alpine Club in Colorado.

Hobnailed boots like the flimsy pair Durrance was stuck with during the first part of the 1939 expedition.

Author's Note

Mountain climbers have a complicated relationship with death.

In the spring of 2018, while I was researching this book, I went to the annual conference of the American Alpine Club in Boston. Every year, the dinner opens with a ritual that's either touching or macabre, depending on your point of view. The president of the AAC stands on stage and asks for a moment of silence for all the club members who have died during the year.

It's not as dramatic as it sounds. Many of the souls on the list have departed peacefully in their sleep. But inevitably, some have been smothered in avalanches, battered in free fall, or frozen into the side of a ridge at 25,000 feet.

Climbers are a community of people who find their greatest joy amid great danger. That paradox fascinates sea level–bound observers—myself included. Reporters, acquaintances, often spouses, all want to know *why*? Life is a precious thing; why risk it in pursuit of something that is, in Francis Younghusband's words, "no use at all"?

Rand Herron, a musical prodigy and lover of mountains who climbed on Nanga Parbat with Fritz Wiessner in 1932, thought the question missed the point. The risk of death wasn't just something to be tolerated in order to unlock the rewards of climbing. It was part of the reward itself. "Although we climbers usually don't admit it," he wrote, "we are always more or less conscious that the strange and irresistible call of the mountains is also a call towards the end of life. And for that very reason we love them all the more, and find their call more sublime. Our secret heart's desire is that our end should be in them." In one of the more poignant ironies in mountaineering history, Herron survived Nanga Parbat and fell 300 feet to his death trying to climb an Egyptian pyramid on the way home.

He died doing what he loved. That's the knee-jerk response to a death in the mountains (and even on an ancient man-made tomb). No doubt it's what Art Gilkey's parents tried to tell themselves. It's a cliché, and it smacks of rationalization. But maybe there are people—like Herron—who can say it and truly mean it.

After all, when viewed from a remove (from a mountaintop, you could say), 80-odd years of life on this Earth is a slim allotment. Maybe the risk of spending it too cautiously outweighs the risk of ending it early. From this vantage point, climbing is the romantic hero's alternative to a life of quiet desperation. "Better to take risks . . . than die within from rot," said Charlie Houston.

At the logical end of that approach to life stands Alex Honnold, who seems to hold his own time on Earth so lightly he wouldn't notice it slipping from his hands. "We're all going to die eventually," he says in *Free Solo*, the film about his unprotected climb up the 3,000-foot wall known as El Capitan. "Soloing just makes it more immediate. You accept the fact that if anything goes wrong, you're going to die. And that's that."

At the AAC dinner, Honnold attracted little congregations wherever he went. I don't think he's especially tall, but I picture him surrounded by people gazing up in awe. I suspect we look up to him not just because we revere what he does on a cliff face but because we expect something exceptional from him on ordinary terrain. After all, liberation from the greatest fear of all should liberate a person from all the daily fears that constrict our lives: *Can I finish this author's note on time? Will it be good enough? Am I good enough—to warrant affection from friends, colleagues, spouse, kids? Good enough to justify my 80-odd years?*

Climbers often talk about finding freedom from ambivalence and self-doubt in the mountains—a Buddhist-like presence in the moment. The climber and photographer

Galen Rowell says it's that feeling, even more than the summit quest, that drives climbers into the mountains. They crave moments when the task becomes so difficult it demands total concentration. "No room exists for such normal mental activities as time measurement or self-contemplation," Rowell says. "Consciousness becomes a smooth, purposeful stream of energy fitted to the task . . . No random thoughts block the flow between body and mind." Nirvana in the Death Zone.

In expedition books, the mountains often appear as a kind of sacred ground that offers a glimpse of a better way to live. They are a world apart, an antidote to civilization and its poisons. Houston said climbing stripped away everything inessential and revealed the "core of life itself."

But to think of the mountains as an escape from the strivings of civilized life is to romanticize what happens there. There's another kind of ambivalence that follows climbers up the slopes, and those with a gift for introspection talk about it a lot. Hours before the British climber Joe Simpson shattered his knee and began his famous battle for survival in the Andes, he and his partner, Simon Yates, stood on the summit of Peru's Siula Grande. Simpson felt a moment of elation that was quickly replaced by disappointment. It was an "anticlimax," he says, part of a never-ending cycle of pursuit with no satisfaction in sight. "If you succeed with one dream," he says in *Touching the Void*, "you come back to square one and it's not long before you're conjuring up another, slightly harder, a bit more ambitious—a bit more dangerous."

That doesn't sound like freedom. It's a high-stakes version of the rat race, set against a skyline of snow-covered peaks. Dee Molenaar wrestled with it all the way up the Abruzzi Ridge. By the end, he just wanted to go home and be "ordinary." I think Charlie Houston struggled with this tension, too. He insisted that mountaineering was about the process, not the goal—the struggle against the elements, the personal bonds forged at opposite ends of a rope. Yet people who knew him remember him as a fiercely competitive man. And K2 lost its magic for him when the Italians won the race to the top.

So maybe the ridges of the great peaks aren't routes to enlightenment, and the people who risk their lives there don't qualify as gurus. Climbers carry the restlessness of their workaday lives with them into the mountains.

But that's what makes their project so fascinating—and no matter what Younghusband says—relevant. Climbing is life with the stakes vividly defined and dramatically high, and that's why the people in this book have meant so much to me over the last year and a half.

After his pioneering climb up the west ridge of Everest in 1963, Tom Hornbein decided he had been looking for something the mountain couldn't provide. The achievement left him grasping toward a revelation that was probably more valuable than anything else he took home with him. "What possible difference could climbing Everest make? . . . Was I any greater for having stood on the highest place on Earth? . . . It is strange how when a dream is fulfilled there is little left but doubt."

That's an experience anyone can relate to. A book begins as a dream. It appears bound, reviewed, maybe even honored by awards committees. The author looks around, the dream fulfilled, wondering why the blank page still looks intimidating. Goals recede from accomplishments. The summit achieved is somehow less than the summit pursued. Maybe it occurs to us that the only real progress is a deeper investment in the sound of a new sentence read aloud or the feel of rock under the fingertips. And maybe that's what Charlie Houston was searching for on K2—"the core of life itself."

Sources

BOOKS

Ata-Ullah, Mohammad. *Citizen of Two Worlds.* New York: Harper & Brothers, 1960.

Bates, Robert H. *The Love of Mountains Is Best: Climbs and Travels from K2 to Kathmandu.* Portsmouth, NH: Peter E. Randall, 1994.

Buhl, Hermann. *Nanga Parbat Pilgrimage.* New York: Penguin Books, 1982.

Conefrey, Mick. *The Ghosts of K2: The Epic Saga of the First Ascent.* London: One World, 2015.

Curran, Jim. *K2: The Story of the Savage Mountain.* Seattle: The Mountaineers, 1995.

_____. *K2: Triumph and Tragedy.* Boston: Houghton Mifflin, 1987.

De Filippi, Filippo. *Karakoram and Western Himalaya 1909: An Account of the Expedition of H.R.H. Prince Luigi Amedeo of Savoy, Duke of the Abruzzi.* New York: E. P. Dutton and Company, 1912.

Fladt, Christiane. *And Death Walks with Them: Above Eight Thousand Metres with Pakistani Porters from Shimshal.* Oxford: Oxford University Press, 2017.

Galbraith, John Kenneth. *A Life in Our Times: Memoirs.* New York: Ballantine, 1982.

Herzog, Maurice. *Annapurna: The Epic Account of a Himalayan Conquest—and Its Harrowing Aftermath.* New York: Lyons Press, 1997.

Hillary, Edmund. *High Adventure: The True Story of the First Ascent of Everest.* Oxford: Oxford University Press, 2003.

Hornbein, Thomas F. *Everest: The West Ridge.* Seattle: The Mountaineers, 1980.

House, Steve. *Beyond the Mountain.* Ventura, CA: Patagonia Books, 2009.

Houston, Charles S. *Going High: The Story of Man and Altitude.* Burlington, VT: Charles S. Houston, M.D. and The American Alpine Club, 1980.

Houston, Charles, David E. Harris, and Ellen J. Zeman. *Going Higher: Oxygen, Man, and Mountains.* Seattle: The Mountaineers, 2005.

Houston, Charles S., and Robert H. Bates. *Five Miles High: The Thrilling True Story of the First American Expedition to K2.* New York: Lyons Press, 2000.

_____. *K2: The Savage Mountain*. Guilford, CT: Lyons Press, 2000.

Isserman, Maurice, and Stewart Weaver. *Fallen Giants: A History of Himalayan Mountaineering from the Age of Empire to the Age of Extremes*. New Haven, CT: Yale University Press, 2008.

Jones, Chris. *Climbing in North America*. Berkeley and Los Angeles: University of California Press, 1976.

Jordan, Jennifer. *The Last Man on the Mountain: The Death of an American Adventurer on K2*. New York: W. W. Norton & Company, 2010.

Kauffman, Andrew J., and William L. Putnam. *K2: The 1939 Tragedy: The Full Story of the Ill-Fated Wiessner Expedition*. Seattle: The Mountaineers, 1992.

McDonald, Bernadette. *Brotherhood of the Rope: The Biography of Charles Houston*. Seattle: The Mountaineers, 2007.

McDonald, Bernadette, and John Amatt, eds. *Voices from the Summit: The World's Greatest Mountaineers on the Future of Climbing*. New York: National Geographic, 2000.

Molenaar, Dee. *Memoirs of a Dinosaur Mountaineer*. Dee Molenaar, 2007.

Neale, Jonathan. *Tigers of the Snow: How One Fateful Climb Made the Sherpas Mountaineering Legends*. New York: St. Martin's Press, 2002.

Petzoldt, Patricia. *On Top of the World: My Adventures with My Mountain Climbing Husband.* New York: Thomas Crowell, 1953.

Price, Larry. *Mountains and Man: A Study of Process and Environment.* Berkeley: University of California Press, 1981.

Rebuffat, Gaston. *Starlight and Storm: The Conquest of the Great North Faces of the Alps.* New York: Modern Library, 1999.

Ridgeway, Rick. *The Last Steps: The American Ascent of K2.* Seattle: The Mountaineers, 1980.

Ringholz, Raye Carleson. *On Belay! The Life of Legendary Mountaineer Paul Petzoldt.* Seattle: The Mountaineers, 1997.

Roberts, David. *Moments of Doubt and Other Mountaineering Writings.* Seattle: The Mountaineers, 1986.

Rowell, Galen. *In the Throne Room of the Mountain Gods.* New York: Random House, 1986.

Schoening, Peter. *K2 1953.* Estate of Peter K. Schoening, 2004.

Simpson, Joe. *Dark Shadows Falling.* Seattle: The Mountaineers, 1997.

_____. *This Game of Ghosts.* Seattle: The Mountaineers, 1995.

Tasker, Joe. *Savage Arena.* New York: St. Martin's Press, 1982.

Viesturs, Ed, with David Roberts. *K2: Life and Death on the World's Most Dangerous Mountain.* New York: Broadway Books, 2009.

West, John B. *High Life: A History of High-Altitude Physiology and Medicine.* New York: Springer, 1998.

Wyss-Dunant, Edward. "Acclimatisation." In *The Mountain World*, edited by Marcel Kurz. London: George Allen & Unwin, 1953.

Zuckerman, Peter, and Amanda Padoan. *Buried in the Sky: The Extraordinary Story of the Sherpa Climbers on K2's Deadliest Day.* New York: W. W. Norton & Company, 2012.

MAGAZINE ARTICLES AND BLOGS

Arnette, Alan. "Why K2 Will Never Become Everest." *The Blog.* June 12, 2016. http://www.alanarnette.com/blog/2016/06/12/k2-will-never-become-everest/.

Bates, Robert H. "The Fight for K2." *American Alpine Journal,* 1954.

_____. "We Met Death on K2." *Saturday Evening Post,* December 5 and 12, 1953.

Bates, Robert H., and Robert B. Forbes. "Arthur K. Gilkey, 1926–1953: In Memoriam." *American Alpine Journal,* 1954.

Boardman, Peter. "Fight for Life on the Savage Mountain." *Observer Magazine,* February 15, 1981.

Clark, Edie. "One Last Mountain to Climb." *Yankee* magazine, May 1997.

Cranmer, Chappel, and Fritz Wiessner. "The Second American Expedition to K2." *American Alpine Journal,* 1940.

Cromwell, Eaton. "Spring Skiing in the Vale of Kashmir." *Appalachia,* December 1940.

Dornan, David. "An Interview with Fritz Wiessner." *Ascent*, Vol. 1, No. 3, May 1969.

Fedarko, Kevin. "The Mountain of Mountains." *Outside*, November 1, 2003.

House, William P. "K2-1938." *American Alpine Journal*, 1939.

Houston, Charles. "A Reconnaissance of K2, 1938." *Himalayan Journal*, Vol. 11, 1939.

_____. "Death in High Places." *American Alpine Journal*, 1987.

Roberts, David. "The K2 Mystery." *Outside*, October 1984.

Sheldon, George. "Lost behind the Ranges." *Saturday Evening Post*, March 16, 1940.

Streather, H. R. A. "Third American Karakoram Expedition 1953." *Himalyan Journal*, Vol. 18, 1954.

Swenson, Steve. "K2: The Mountaineer's Mountain, Part One" and "K2 Mountain Profile: Part Two (1974–2012)." *Alpinist* (37, 38), Winter 2011–2012, Spring 2012.

Terrell, Karen Molenaar. "Children of the Belay." *Newsweek*, November 2, 2006. Posted 2017 at https://1953k2expedition.wordpress.com/2017/07/17/children-of-the-belay/.

Wiessner, Fritz. "The K2 Expedition of 1939." *Appalachia*, June 1956.

Worrall, Simon. "Why K2 Brings Out the Best and Worst in Those Who Climb It." *National Geographic*, December 13, 2015.

NEWSPAPER ARTICLES

"Americans Reach 25,000-Foot Mark on Godwin Austen."
Boston Globe, August 16, 1953.

"Climbing Mount Everest Is Work for Supermen." *New York
Times*, March 18, 1923.

"Columbia U. Student Killed in Attempt to Scale Himalaya
Peak." *New York Daily News*, September 2, 1953.

"Earth's Third Pole—Everest." *New York Times*, May 31, 1953.

"Houston Expects a K2 Conquest without Oxygen." *Boston
Globe*, August 30, 1953.

"In the Northwest: Pete Schoening to Be Forever
Remembered for the Belay." *Seattle Post-Intelligencer*,
September 23, 2004.

"Iowan Is Trying to Climb Second-Tallest Mountain." *Des
Moines Tribune*, July 16, 1953.

"K2 Finally Surrenders Hub Climber's Remains." *Boston
Globe*, July 28, 2002.

"Letter Clarifies Accounts of Arthur Gilkey's Fatal Accident."
Ames Daily Tribune, September 12, 1953.

"Men against the Mightiest Peaks." *New York Times Magazine*,
April 17, 1938.

"Pete Schoening, 77, Accomplished Climber, Is Dead." *New
York Times*, September 27, 2004.

"Pete 'The Belay' Schoening." *The Telegraph*, October 4, 2004.

"Three New Englanders Near World's 2nd Highest Peak."
Boston Globe, July 8, 1953.

"U.S. Climbers Move Up K2." *Newport Daily News*,
August 6, 1953.

"Why They Climb and Climb and Climb." *New York Times
Magazine*, April 10, 1960.

VIDEO

Beyond the Edge. Leanne Pooley, dir. General Film
Corporation, 2013. Film.

Exploring the Heights. Charles Houston. Film.

Ghosts of K2. Mick Conefrey. BBC, 2013. Film.

"Remembering Charles Houston." *Bill Moyers Journal*.
October 9, 2009. PBS Television.

The Summit. Nick Ryan, dir. IFC Films, 2012. Film.

ARCHIVAL SOURCES

Andrew John Kauffman II Collection. American Alpine Club
Library.

Charles Houston Papers. University of California San Diego.

Charles Houston K2 1938–1953 Expedition Correspondence.
AAC Library.

Charles Houston K2 expedition diary, 1938. Private collection,
Greg Glade.

Dee Molenaar K2 expedition diary, 1953. University of
Washington Special Collections.

First American Karakoram Expedition, 1938. Expedition letters. AAC Library.

George Sheldon K2 expedition diary, 1939. Kauffman Collection, Box 2, Folder 10. AAC Library.

Jack Durrance K2 expedition diary, 1939. Kauffman Collection, Box 2, Folder 4. AAC Library.

K2 Expedition Tape transcript. August 16, 1953. AAC Library.

Second American Karakoram Expedition, 1939. Expedition letters. AAC Library.

Third American Karakoram Expedition, 1953. Expedition Letters. AAC Library.

AUTHOR INTERVIEWS

Bates, Gail. February 22, 2018.

Bell, Carolyn. February 13, 2018.

Bell, Ginny. February 14, 2018.

Houston, Robin. January 26, 2018.

Hornbein, Thomas. January 25, 2018. Including email correspondence, January–November. 2018.

Jertz, Lisa. December 16, 2017. Including email correspondence, December 2017–November 2018

O'Brien, Vanessa. August 7, 2018.

Powers, Phil. August 24, 2017.

Schoening, Mark. December 19, 2017. Including email correspondence, December 2017–November 2018.

Source Notes

PROLOGUE

"Two men reached the top.": Houston and Bates, *Savage Mountain*, 158.

"I'm all right. . . .": Houston and Bates, 162.

"It's sure to clear up . . .": Houston and Bates, 163.

"sometimes bits of clot break off . . .": Houston and Bates, 163.

CHAPTER 1

"Most mountains are of the Earth.": Galbraith, *A Life in Our Times*, 335.

"Travelers are often attacked . . .": quoted in Houston et al., *Going Higher*, 83.

"Men's bodies become feverish . . .": quoted in West, *High Life*, 7.

"Life there is impossible": Wyss-Dunant, "Acclimatisation," 113.

"If I am asked what is the use of climbing": quoted in Isserman and Weaver, *Fallen Giants*, 84.

"Who first faces and triumphs . . .": quoted in Isserman and Weaver, 86.

"Because it's there.": "Climbing Mount Everest Is Work for Supermen."

"[Mankind] has the notion . . .": "Men against the Mightiest Peaks," 11.

"Is it not better to take risks . . .": Houston expedition diary, 1938.

CHAPTER 2

wastebasket scene described in Bates, *Love of Mountains*, 101.

"set for life": McDonald, *Brotherhood of the Rope*, 121.

"Wiessner's idea . . .": quoted in Viesturs, *K2: Life and Death*, 90.

"Just the bare bones of a name": Fosco Maraini, quoted in Curran, *K2: The Story of the Savage Mountain*, 30.

statistics on the number of successful Everest attempts: Himalayan Database: The Expedition Archives of Elizabeth Hawley, Himalayandatabase.com.

K2 summit attempts and deaths: Arnette, "Why K2 Will Never Become Everest."

"these are not mountains like other mountains": De Filippi, *Karakoram and Western Himalaya*, 235.

"amateurs": Viesturs, *K2: Life and Death*, 95; according to biographer Raye Ringholz, when Petzoldt was on his way to K2, he discovered a memo at the AAC calling him a "Wyoming packer and guide" and questioning whether he would fit in with the rest of the expedition; it didn't make him happy; *On Belay!*, 86.

CHAPTER 3

Bates describes their food, supplies, and testing methods in Houston and Bates, *Five Miles High*, 33–38, 356–352; and Bates, *Love of Mountains*, 107.

"At every step the rope contraption . . .": Houston and Bates, *Five Miles High*, 127.

"It was like something from another world, . . .": Houston and Bates, 151.

"Bob and I very mad": Houston expedition diary, June 22, 1938.

"Instantly our attitude to the mountain changed": Houston and Bates, *Five Miles High*, 210.

CHAPTER 4

"ironware": Houston and Bates, *Five Miles High*, 230.

"Dreading days work . . .": Houston expedition diary, July 13, 1938.

"Just like Nanga Parbat": Bates, *Love of Mountains*, 136.

1934 Nanga Parbat disaster described in Neale, *Tigers of the Snow*, 144–193; Isserman and Weaver, *Fallen Giants*, 171–182.

"We now felt further removed . . .": Houston and Bates, *Five Miles High*, 265–266.

"I struggled on . . .": Houston and Bates, 278.

"let our puny bodies . . .": Houston and Bates, 279.

CHAPTER 5

Houston's dinner with Durrance described in Jordan, *Last Man*, 94–95, and Durrance expedition diary, March 21, 1939.

Wolfe made the "good sense" comment in the letter to his brother: quoted in Jordan, *Last Man*, 83.

debate over two-way radios discussed in Kauffman and Putnam, *K2: 1939 Tragedy*, 94, 154; Wiessner said he rejected radios for "ideological reasons," but in 1939 they were also bulky and not often used on big expeditions.

condition of the porters described in Second Expedition letter #6, June 4, 1939; Sheldon describes the general condition of the porters in his letter to the AAC but leaves out details about their failure to provide goggles.

"Get up and get moving.": Jordan, *Last Man*, 132.

"A trip like this . . .": quoted in Jordan, 131.

CHAPTER 6

Movements on the mountain were documented by the AAC from the climbers' reports, "Movements of Climbers on K2," Kauffman Collection.

"There is no expression to describe . . .": Durrance expedition diary, June 7, 1939.

"I just wanted to see . . .": quoted in Kauffman and Putnam, *K2: 1939 Tragedy*, 82.

"This trip & mountaineering . . .": Durrance expedition diary, June 16, 1939.

"Dudley is up on the mountain . . .": Second Expedition letter #7, June 14, 1939.

Sheldon wrote about his fear during the storm in "Lost behind the Ranges," 126.

"My attitude about K2 . . .": quoted in Jordan, *Last Man*, 157.

CHAPTER 7

"Tony and I will remain in II . . .": letter quoted in full in Kauffman and Putnam, *K2: 1939 Tragedy*, 91.

"I am very disappointed in you.": Durrance expedition diary, July 2, 1939.

"We move only as puppets . . .": Durrance, July 2, 1939.

"Lo and behold, Fritz came forth . . .": Durrance, July 10, 1939.

"Pop Sahib [Cromwell] declares he is now used up . . .": Durrance, July 10, 1939.

"in reserve": from Wiessner's diary, quoted in Jordan, *Last Man*, 168; according to Cranmer and Trench, Wiessner didn't keep a journal on the mountain; his diary was filled in from memory after he left the mountain.

"It is unfair to take a man along . . .": This appears at the end of Durrance's diary, probably written at Base Camp more than a week later. Durrance expedition diary, 1939.

CHAPTER 8

For Tendrup, Tsering, Kitar, and Phinsoo, there are almost no written accounts from Sherpa climbers in this era and few interviews, which makes it hard to know exactly what they were thinking; the story of what happened at Camp VI comes from the Western climbers' accounts of Tendrup's story.

"It's hopeless, Fritz . . .": quoted in Jordan, *Last Man*, 182.

"Salvage all the tents . . .": Durrance expedition diary, 1939, July 18.

"Tomorrow": "Interview with Fritz Wiessner," 19. Years later, Lama told the Austrian mountaineer and author Kurt Maix that Wiessner was crazy: "I never see someone climb like he. I no see nothing—it night. But Wiessner say 'it very bright.' Maybe he see with fingertips." Kauffman Collection, Box 2, Folder 11.

"If we get up": Andrew Kauffman's notes from interview with Durrance, Dec. 7, 1986. Kauffman Collection, Box 2, Folder 12.

CHAPTER 9

For Wiessner's actions and reactions high on the mountain over the next couple of days the only source is Wiessner himself. He wrote later in his diary, "I cannot understand why our Sherpas . . . had not come. I also wondered where was Jack"; Wiessner diary, July 22, 1939. From partial transcript in Kauffman Collection, Box 2, Folder 6.

"It was obvious to us . . .": Wiessner diary, July 22, 1939.

Tendrup's account of what happened at Camp VI and above comes from recollections by Durrance and Cromwell; see Durrance expedition diary, July 24, 1939.

Many people have since speculated about the interaction between Wiessner and Wolfe at Camp VII. Durrance, at Base Camp while Wiessner was making his last-ditch attempt to look for the missing climbers, wondered about it in his diary. He found it impossible to believe that Wiessner would consider taking Wolfe to the summit after their problems coming down. He also wondered why, after seeing Camp VII, Wiessner would not assume Camp VI had been stripped as well. Durrance, August 5.

CHAPTER 10

"Thank God you're alive!": Kauffman and Putnam, *K2: 1939 Tragedy*, 124.

Cromwell described Wiessner's rant to Sheldon when he met up with him in Askole. Sheldon diary, July 31, 1939.

"Maybe the Gods will be with me . . .": Wiessner diary, July 24, 1939.

"Good luck for me to have a man like Pasang left": Wiessner diary, July 27.

"I ran out of matches": the account of this encounter is at least third-hand, from Wiessner and Durrance via Tsering, who heard it from Kikuli. See Durrance expedition diary, August 2, 1939; Wiessner diary, August 2, 1939.

Durrance noted the porters' reaction to his mood in his diary, July 30.

"neither our brave Dudley Wolfe. . .": Cranmer and Wiessner, "Second American Expedition to K2."

CHAPTER 11

Bates describes the preparations at the Houston home in Houston and Bates, *Savage Mountain*, 54–58.

Houston told Jennifer Jordan about his encounter with Durrance, in Jordan, *Last Man*, 270.

"Fritz and I part ways": Durrance expedition diary, September 20, 1939.

Mason's criticism of Wiessner is in "Himalayan Accidents in 1939," *Himalayan Journal*, Vol. 12, 1940.

"Wiessner, with Wolfe behind him . . .": quoted in Roberts, *Moments of Doubt*, 179.

"A Himalayan mountain is like war . . .": from a letter to Wolfe's brother Clifford Smith, quoted in Jordan, *Last Man*, 214; also mentioned in Sheldon diary, July 31, 1939.

"weak administration": "Report on the 1939 American Alpine Club Karakoram Expedition." Kauffman Collection, Box 2, Folder 13.

"Wiessner is to blame . . .": letter to friend and climbing partner Bradford Washburn, quoted in Viesturs, *K2: Life and Death*, 175.

"There is plenty of swanking . . . ": Schoening letter to parents, May 21, 1953, in Schoening, *K2 1953*.

"When the low clouds are grey and stormy . . .": letter to Bates, October 25, 1942, quoted in Isserman and Weaver, *Fallen Giants*, 226.

"FOR THE AMERICANS, K-2 MUST DO": *Boston Globe*, January 14, 1953.

"We will try to let nothing short of a world war stop us": Houston to AAC president Henry Hall, February 27, 1952, quoted in Isserman and Weaver, *Fallen Giants*, 306.

"Be careful": Molenaar, *Memoirs*, 127.

CHAPTER 12

The view of Nanga Parbat from the plane is described by Ata-Ullah in *Citizen of Two Worlds*, 234.

"Pakistan *zinzabad*! America *zinzabad*!": Houston and Bates, *Savage Mountain*, 128.

"A conquest of K2 by Americans . . .": *Boston Globe*, January 14, 1953.

"Now K2 is highest unclimbed mtn. on earth . . .": Molenaar expedition diary, 1953, June 2.

"*saf pani lao* . . .": Molenaar diary, 1953.

"Nothing on the whole planet matches it": Rick Ridgeway, one of the first Americans to summit K2, quoted in Fedarko, "Mountain of Mountains."

"Looks very steep and rugged": Molenaar expedition diary, June 19, 1953.

Schoening describes the first night in Base Camp in a letter to his family, June 18, in *K2 1953*; he describes porters building windbreaks from rocks and huddling under tarps at night, eating cold food since they had no fuel to build fires.

CHAPTER 13

"Too close": Molenaar expedition diary, June 30, 1953.

"playing sick": Schoening's expedition diary is reprinted in full in his self-published book, *K2 1953*; this entry is from July 1. As with the Sherpas, it's impossible to say for sure what the Hunzas thought or felt on the expedition, as the only sources we have are from the perspective of the Western climbers.

"Thinking of long climb ahead . . .": Molenaar expedition diary, July 2, 1953.

"Would you fellows mind . . .": Houston and Bates, *Savage Mountain*, 122.

"Come on up . . .": Houston and Bates, 122.

"Sunshine, warmth make attitude entirely different . . .": Molenaar expedition diary, July 17, 1953.

Houston describes the eerie sight of the bundles left at Camp VI in Houston and Bates, *Savage Mountain*, 140; Bates describes it in a recorded conversation the climbers had when they got back to Base Camp, reconstructing the last days on the mountain. K2 Expedition tape transcript.

CHAPTER 14

"Pretty slippery spot": Houston and Bates, *Savage Mountain*, 144.

"In an hour or two . . .": Herzog, *Annapurna*, 206.

Herzog, on his tour in the U.S., told the *New York Times*, "I lost a great deal [on Annapurna], but I found many marvelous things that had been unknown to me. I used to think that the chief thing was to be strong, that strength came before everything else." *New York Times Book Review*, March 22, 1953, 12.

"Bringing an injured man down K2 . . .": Molenaar expedition diary, July 28, 1953.

"at all costs": Molenaar diary, July 31.

"Charlie is like a mother . . .": Schoening expedition diary, July 30, 1953.

Schoening describes the discovery of the Camp VIII site in his diary, July 31. The two days Schoening and Gilkey spent on the dangerous ice and snow slope between VII and VIII took an enormous toll on them. Stoic as always, Schoening merely writes, "Art is quite irritable and maybe myself."

CHAPTER 15

vicious monsoon season in Pakistan in 1953: Rowell, *Throne Room*, 228; "Monsoon rain in Lower Sindh (1950–2011)," PakistanWeatherPortal.com.

"Party again together! . . .": Molenaar expedition diary, August 2, 1953.

"the wonderful life ahead . . .": Molenaar diary, August 3.

"Should we get out of the tent . . .": Houston describes the tent collapsing in Houston and Bates, *Savage Mountain*, 159; also in K2 Expedition Tape transcript.

"Hello Base Camp . . .": Houston and Bates, *Savage Mountain*, 155.

"What's the use?": "Iowan Is Trying to Climb Second-Tallest Mountain," *Des Moines Tribune*, July 16, 1953.

CHAPTER 16

Schoening insisted all his life that it had been possible to get Art down alive. "It would have taken longer than descending by ourselves and frostbite would have been more severe," he wrote in *K2 1953*. "But based on experience doing rescues on steep terrain, I believe we could have done it." Pete's son Mark Schoening pointed this out in an email exchange with me. "Almost makes you want to try harder at whatever it is we're doing right now, doesn't it?" he said.

"I'll be climbing again tomorrow": Houston and Bates, *Savage Mountain*, 177.

"Our present battle . . .": Molenaar expedition diary, 1953, August 8.

"*Survival* is the only term suitable . . .": Wyss-Dunant, "Acclimatisation," 113.

As Molenaar was speculating about Dudley Wolfe's final days, he wrote, "Any physical exertion at this altitude demands a great deal of will power to even put it into motivation": Molenaar expedition diary, August 6, 1953.

"Terrible thought . . .": Molenaar diary, August 9.

Molenaar's letter to Lee: Molenaar diary, August 9.

"Just fine—just fine": Bates, "The Fight for K2," *American Alpine Journal*, 1954.

"It's pretty desperate . . .": Houston and Bates, *Savage Mountain*, 177–178.

"Hold him! . . .": K2 Expedition Tape transcript; Schoening, *K2 1953*, 204.

CHAPTER 17

All the accounts of the fall are pretty consistent; where there were discrepancies, I tended to rely on the conversation taped at Base Camp on August 16, 1953 (K2 Expedition Tape transcript) because the least time had elapsed since it happened and because they had each other to help recall what happened.

"The violent and numbing reality . . .": Simpson, *This Game of Ghosts*, ch. 16; years later this quote seemed to Molenaar to describe the experience he had on K2. Molenaar, *Memoirs*, 150.

"Goddamn, there goes Bell!": Molenaar, *Memoirs*, 149.

Bates describes his feeling of resignation during the fall in "We Met Death on K2," 61.

"Get your weight off the rope!": Houston and Bates, *Savage Mountain*, 196.

"Who's there?": K2 Expedition Tape transcript, Schoening, *K2 1953*, 208.

"My hands are freezing": Houston and Bates, *Savage Mountain*, 196.

"Where are we? . . .": described in Bates, *Love of Mountains*, 282; Houston and Bates, 198–199; Bates, "We Met Death on K2."

"It was as if the hand of God . . .": Houston and Bates, 210.

"There's no better place to die than K2": Molenaar, *Memoirs*, 151–152.

CHAPTER 18

"How's Pete? . . .": The night with Houston in the tent is described in Houston and Bates, *Savage Mountain*, 212–213.

"Poor Art!": Molenaar expedition diary, August 11, 1953; Houston and Bates's expedition book, *Savage Mountain*, doesn't mention this scene at all, and none of the climbers were able to talk about it with each other until years later.

"Thank god": Ata-Ullah, *Citizen of Two Worlds*, 260.

Houston describes his moment of despair at the top of House's Chimney in Mick Conefrey's excellent film *Ghosts of K2*; this may have been the first time Houston told this story publicly.

"It's the deepest experience . . .": K2 Expedition Tape transcript, *K2 1953*, 212.

"We started as strangers . . .": Bates, "We Met Death on K2," *Saturday Evening Post*, December 12, 1953, 166.

EPILOGUE

Pete Schoening's wedding: email from Pete's daughter Lisa Jertz, November 2, 2018.

Molenaar describes Lee's request for a divorce in a single sentence at the end of his expedition diary, September 10.

Bates noted his visit to Gilkey's parents in a letter to Henry Hall, January 14, 1954, AAC Library Archives.

"Nothing I can tell you . . .": "Letter Clarifies Accounts of Arthur Gilkey's Fatal Accident," *Ames Daily Tribune*, September 12, 1953, p. 1

"It's a savage mountain . . .": Conefrey, *Ghosts of K2*, 273.

"There are other hills . . .": Houston letter to British climber Eric Shipton, August 4, 1954, quoted in Conefrey, 234.

Houston's amnesia episode following news of the Italian expedition is described in McDonald, *Brotherhood of the Rope*, 137–139, and Conefrey, 233–234.

"It is now one of the great legends . . .": quoted in Fedaro, "Mountain of Mountains."

"As the prime mover . . .": afterword to Houston and Bates, *Savage Mountain*, quoted in McDonald, *Brotherhood of the Rope*, 139.

"courage and their perseverance": *New York Times*, August 21, 1954, 16.

"blow to the ego or pride . . .": Molenaar expedition diary, August 3, 1953.

"They failed in the most beautiful way . . .": quoted in obituary "Charles S. Houston, Who Led a Failed Himalayan Climb, Dies at 96," *New York Times*, September 30, 2009.

Photo Credits

Photos ©: x: Urban Golob/Alamy Images; xiii, xiv: Peter K. Schoening Mountaineering Archives LLC; 1: Henry S. Hall Jr. American Alpine Club Library; 4–5: Imagex/Depositphotos; 10: Illustrated London News Ltd/Mary Evans Picture Library; 14: The Picture Art Collection/Alamy Stock Photo; 19: DeAgostini/Getty Images; 21: Frank S. Smythe/Getty Images; 28: Henry S. Hall Jr. American Alpine Club Library; 30: Ed Webster Collection; 35: Ed Webster Collection; 39: Universal Images Group North America LLC/DeAgostini/Alamy Stock Photo; 44–45: Ed Webster Collection; 51: Henry S. Hall Jr. American Alpine Club Library; 56: News Photograph/Ed Webster Collection; 59, 62, 63, 66, 69, 74, 76, 81, 86: Henry S. Hall Jr. American Alpine Club Library; 89: Courtesy Fritz Wiessner Family Collection; 94: Universal Images Group North America LLC/DeAgostini/Alamy Stock Photo; 98: Henry S. Hall Jr. American Alpine Club Library; 101: Courtesy Fritz Wiessner Family Collection; 109, 118, 123: Henry S. Hall Jr. American Alpine Club Library; 125 top and bottom: Dee Molenaar; 128: Henry S. Hall Jr. American Alpine Club Library; 133: Dee Molenaar; 138: Peter K. Schoening Mountaineering Archives LLC; 140: Dee Molenaar; 143, 146: Peter K. Schoening Mountaineering Archives LLC; 148: Dee Molenaar; 152: Charlie Houston; 155: Dee Molenaar; 157, 160: Peter K. Schoening Mountaineering Archives LLC; 161: Charlie Houston; 165: Peter K. Schoening Mountaineering Archives LLC; 169: adoc-photos/Getty Images; 172, 178: Peter K. Schoening Mountaineering Archives LLC; 182: Dee Molenaar; 186, 193: Peter K.

Acknowledgments

I owe a debt of gratitude first to the family members of the '53 climbers, many of whom would not exist if it weren't for Pete Schoening and his ice axe. They held a reunion in 2006 and named themselves the Children of the Belay. I'm especially grateful to Lisa Jertz, Pete's daughter, who shared memories of her father as well as his photographs, introduced me to a host of climbers, and guided me through the AAC annual dinner in Boston. Gail Bates, who was a remarkable 100 years old when I met her at that dinner, spent two hours telling me stories of adventures with her husband, Bob. Robin Houston, Mark Schoening, Carolyn Bell, Ginny Bell, and Karen Molenaar Terrell also shared their valuable time with me. Andy and Polly Wiessner graciously shared their father's photos.

Tom Hornbein deserves a special thanks for his generous spirit, his remembrances of the climbers, and his expert eye on a version of this book. He's been an inspiration to many people, and I'm lucky to count myself one of them. Vanessa O'Brien, who has stood at the top of K2, spent hours on the phone walking me up and down the Abruzzi Ridge. That is as close as I'll get to climbing it.

Katie Sauter and her assistant, Eric Rueth, at the AAC Library expertly fielded my pesky requests on two visits to their rich cache of slides, diaries, correspondence, and hob-nailed climbing boots. Heather Smedberg at UC San Diego helped me sort through Charlie Houston's papers from a distance. Greg Glade, a friend of Charlie's and owner of Top of the World Books, shared other hard-to-find sources. Maurice Isserman graciously gave me guidance on research and a host of other questions. Ken Yager at the Yosemite Climbing Association went out of his way to find photos of vintage climbing gear. Ed Webster emerged from Antarctica just in time to share memories and photos of Fritz Wiessner, Paul Petzoldt, and Bill House.

Amanda Shih at Scholastic shepherded this book with a wise, confident hand. Miriam Altshuler, who is simply the best agent ever, shepherded me.

▲

Thanks to Laura McCaffrey, Leda Schubert, and Daphne Kalmar for their advice and counsel, and for making a lonely pursuit so much less so. Laura's attention to the words on the page was essential, as always. Elizabeth Ward read with the expert devotion she has brought to countless pieces of writing since she first made me revise while looking over her shoulder. (When was that, again?)

Thanks to Jill and Richard for their investment in the manuscript, and to Estie and Richard for the care they invested in me. Thanks to Zoe and Finn for continuing to fill me with optimism for the future, and to Jill, who makes so many things possible in the present.

About the Author

TOD OLSON is the author of the narrative nonfiction series LOST® and the historical fiction series How to Get Rich. He holds an MFA from Vermont College of the Fine Arts and lives in Vermont with his family, his mountain bike, and his electric reclining chair.